We are Ripple Effect

Theatre of Witness in Northern Ireland

By Teya Sepinuck

with

*Anne Walker
Fionnbharr Ó HÁgain
James Greer
Jon McCourt
Kathleen Gillespie
Robin Young
Syd Trotter
Therese McCann
Victoria Geelan
William McKee*

and

Dr Thomas Spiers

Published by The Playhouse

Editor: Siobhan Dignan
Design/Portrait Photography: Mark Willett
Cover Art: Susan Teegen

Copyright © The Playhouse 2023.
All rights reserved.

No part of this book may be reproduced or distributed in any form without prior written permission from the publisher, with the exception of non-commercial uses permitted by UK copyright law.

To seek permission contact:
info@derryplayhouse.com
+44 28 7126 8027
www.derryplayhouse.co.uk

5-7 Artillery St
Derry / Londonderry
BT48 6RG

ISBN 978-1-7393307-0-5

Dedicated to Pauline Ross

Whose vision, dedication, and invitation brought Theatre of Witness to Northern Ireland, nurtured it with love and care, and trusted us all to make magic with these stories.

Your spirit is intertwined in these words.

Contents

Foreword   8
EAMONN DEANE

Genesis   10

Prelude   22

We Carried Your Secrets   24

There Never Was a Beginning, Middle or End   26
FIONNBHARR Ó HÁGAIN

The Dance of Peace   42
ROBIN YOUNG

What Do We Pass from One Generation to the Next?   60
VICTORIA GEELEN

The River   78
JAMES GREER

A Letter to My Grandchild   100
JON MCCOURT

I Once Knew a Girl — 118

Sanctuary — 120
THERESE MCCANN

Ordinary Woman — 138
ANNE WALKER

May He Be an Instrument of Thy Peace — 162
KATHLEEN GILLESPIE

Release — 188

The Eyes that See All — 190
SYD TROTTER

The Man Who Tried to Keep Peace — 204
WILLIAM MCKEE

Coda — 222

Addendum — 224

Thirteen Guiding Principles — 225
TEYA SEPINUCK

Trauma and Re-trauma — 237
DR THOMAS SPIERS

Glossary of Terms — 260

Acknowledgments — 262

Endorsements — 265

Foreword

Eamonn Deane

October 2022. Founder, Holywell Trust, Derry-Londonderry, Northern Ireland

There are many, many books published about peacebuilding. There are all sorts of theories about how to bring an end to conflict. These are important resources.

When you are caught up in the middle of a contested space, when suddenly your life has been changed; when you are faced with events which enrage, destroy, diminish, insult, cause despair and hurt beyond pain - theories and rational explanations do not matter - what are you to do? Breathe deeply, breathe again and again - there is no answer other than to cope for a day, a few days, a week, maybe longer. Gradually, perhaps with the help of friends, you can find someone to lean on, someone to be with you. Maybe you find ways in which to create a bit more space, some more breathing room. You continue to exist. That is not enough.

You may well be like so many others, forever limited by this trauma which defines who you are and how you will interpret the rest of the world. You are silenced. Your most profound hopes, dreams and expectations are laid to waste. The world moves on; contested spaces become more entrenched in your heart, and libraries full of books about peacebuilding are not places you visit.

This book is different. This book is not about theories. This book is about engagement. This book is not about somebody telling you how you should be. This book is about how 'ordinary' people like you were facilitated to tell the world how they are, what violence did to them and still does to them. Further, this book presents us with an insight into how one remarkable woman, Teya Sepinuck, helped people find the medicine in stories of suffering, and by doing so helped transform their own lives and the lives of others in building peace.

Teya has blended her experience as a dramatist, a dancer, a writer, a group facilitator, a mother and a teacher of incredible sensitivity, to develop a way of working with people who have had immensely damaging experiences to find an articulation of those experiences in a theatrical space, a public shared space, and by doing so, find meaning, healing and release.

This is a collection of several individual journeys of people moving from emotional paralysis and the trap of predictability towards wisdom and wholeness.

The courage and commitment of the participants in this process has been remarkable. To each of the individuals who have given so much, I pass on the thanks of a wider community. This process can and will be replicated elsewhere.

Teya's work will continue. It has been an honour and privilege to work alongside her. What has been achieved is quite remarkable.

All of this has been made possible by the foresight, courage and risk-taking of Pauline Ross in her role as Director of The Playhouse. It was Pauline who invited Teya to Derry. We at Holywell Trust were greatly honoured to be invited to be a partner in this process.

The publication of this book marks many years of Pauline Ross' creative endeavours. From the foundation of The Playhouse onwards, she has contributed so much to the city and beyond.

May Pauline have many years in which to reap the rich rewards that her courage and insight deserves.

Eamonn Deane - Eamonn in his role as Director of Holywell Trust was a vital and instrumental partner in Theatre of Witness in Northern Ireland.

Genesis

On a misty Philadelphia day, midway through the pandemic, the faces of nine of the original Theatre of Witness performers from Northern Ireland lit up my computer screen. Gazing at them from more than three thousand miles away, I felt their passion and enthusiasm shine. After thirteen years of performances, workshops and presentations, I was struck by how much they had evolved individually, and as a family of practitioners, since our original Theatre of Witness productions finished touring in 2014.

Now we were together on Zoom, preparing for a series of international workshops, and they were filling me in about the presentations they'd done in schools and community centres. I felt excited by their wise anecdotes and effortless ease with each other. I missed them.

From 2009 to 2014, I had been in residence at The Playhouse in Derry-Londonderry, Northern Ireland, creating original Theatre of Witness productions and films with victims, members of the security forces, ex-paramilitaries and young adults from the next generation. All of whom shared their own true stories of how the Troubles and its aftermath had affected them.

Funded by an EU Peace Grant, thirty performers and I created four productions in which they mined their most complex and traumatic experiences, sharing stories onstage that, for the most part, had been hidden up until then. Each of the productions was performed more than fourteen times throughout the North and across the border. Documentary films made of each continue to be shown in peacebuilding workshops and presentations.

On the Zoom call, the performers exuded confidence and strength. I felt their commitment to continue sharing their Theatre of Witness stories to inspire healing and reconciliation. Relationships between them had blossomed and their positive energy was palpable. I was humbled.

"You have all become such extraordinary peacemakers and teachers. Someone should write a book about you." "There was a pause, and I felt chills all up and down my spine. "Maybe that person is me." Even from another continent across the Atlantic, all these years later, perhaps I could once again be back in the thick of collaboration with them.

When I lived and worked in Northern Ireland, that collaborative creative process had been built on being physically present with each of them, individually and in groups, for hours and hours. Those intimate sessions had allowed me to notice the performers' gestures, breathing, emotional shifts and subtle facial and body cues as I crafted each production. The work grew from our ongoing and deepening relationships. But now I wondered: would I be able to write about them from afar? I had been out of their lives for so many years. Would I know enough?

I found my answer in one of the Theatre of Witness Guiding Principles that underpins the work: *Take the Problem and Make it the Solution*. The 'problem' was that I was unsure if I knew how to write about the performers without being back in Northern Ireland with them. So much time had elapsed, during which we had all grown and had myriad new experiences. They had carried on with the work and I lived an ocean away.

But the 'solution' was that, as an outsider, I could invite the performers to reflect on how the work had grown for them since our last times together. And instead of me sifting their thoughts through my own artistic lens, as I had done when we were creating the production, here I could transcribe their words and ideas and let them stand on their own without a lot of interpretation or contextualisation on my part.

So, I trusted that the excitement I felt when I listened to the participants share on Zoom was an indicator there was a lot of profound wisdom in their thoughts. And I could take a back seat.

My hope is that, in reading the performers' stories about the creation of the productions and the ripples for their lives and others' they've touched in the years that followed, the readers will understand how powerful and extraordinary the connections between them are. The relationships between William and Syd - a former prison governor and an ex-paramilitary prisoner, or Kathleen and Anne - a woman who lost her husband to paramilitary violence and another who had been part of that very paramilitary group, gives so many of us hope.

These unlikely connections formed much of what was innovative and powerful about Theatre of Witness. Even now, more than twelve years postproduction, the ten individuals who have carried on presenting Theatre of Witness continue to surprise workshop participants with their unexpected authentic friendships. Thus, in this book, some of their stories about their relationships overlap. I have chosen to keep them as is, to honour each of their own particular ways of expressing these bonds.

Background
What is Theatre of Witness?

Theatre of Witness is a form of testimonial theatre in which those who have gone through significant life experiences share their true stories onstage. Its purpose is to create a form for audiences to bear witness to issues of suffering, transformation and peace. The work lies at an intersection between art/social change/spirituality/social services/history/and politics.

Theatre of Witness is a modern phenomenon based on the oldest of needs – the need to tell our story, to be listened to, to find healing for ourselves, and for everyone in our ability to empathise, to be generous and find light in the darkest pit.
Eamonn Deane, Founder and former director of Holywell Trust

In these divided times, a story can warm hearts, heal our broken spirits and bring us together for a unified experience. The Theatre of Witness goal is to do just that. To share with us the lived experience of performers whose stories of resilience and transformation address some of society's most complex issues and can reinspire our sense of what is possible. It is built upon one of its Guiding Principles: *Finding the Medicine in the Centre of the Wound* – the place of accountability, strength or transformation.

I developed Theatre of Witness in 1986 after a career in dance, because I was looking to expand my world. I wanted to immerse myself in the lives and stories of people who lived very differently from me. I was ready for new teachers. Teachers who not only had the lived experience of trauma and transformation, but whose sometimes messy and tangled lives embodied new paths to find meaning in one's own life.

From the beginning, I wanted the performers in Theatre of Witness to be the very people whose stories were being told – not actors. I was interested in embodied storytelling as a form of bearing witness for audience members - bearing witness to living/breathing human beings sharing their own vulnerabilities and strength. Where audiences would be inspired to cultivate empathy and to humanise the 'other'.

I wanted to forge a larger collective narrative that brings people together across divides of difference to hear and give presence to personal and communal accounts of suffering, transformation and peace. Thus, while Theatre of Witness is first and foremost an artistic form, it is also a communal spiritual experience of being present and open.

Just as important as the effect on the audience, I was interested in the process of growth and transformation for the performers. What would happen when a group of people who had lived through traumatic experiences became deeply engaged in the Theatre of Witness creative process with each other over time? Especially people from opposing sides of a conflict? The transformation that I have seen occur in almost all of the participants was nothing short of miraculous.

Theatre of Witness Performers

Theatre of Witness isn't created by those who are faint of heart, or who are interested in acting or fame. It is meant to be performed by people who reveal their difficult wounds and memories to help audiences gain insight, strength or healing. Such individuals want to make a difference in the world and believe in the power of going into the darkest regions of their own suffering to bring out the light for all. It is for people who seek to delve into this process as part of a conscious community of practitioners, many of whom come from backgrounds that differ greatly from each other.

Theatre of Witness performers in the US and Poland have included refugees and immigrants, those affected by violence, poverty, conflict and/or racism, survivors and perpetrators of abuse, ex-combatants, police and security forces, teenage runaways, people living with mental and/or physical health issues, elders, healthcare professionals, peacemakers and visionaries. Most of the Theatre productions have been made into documentary films which are available long after the live productions have concluded.

I recently asked some of the Northern Irish performers to describe in their own words what the Theatre of Witness process has meant to them. Interestingly, a common theme that came out was 'magnetisation'. Magnetisation in relation to each other and towards the truth.

Initially, I felt the power of this work in my being. It drew me in like the strongest of magnets, now I don't just feel it, I live and know it. It's the freedom I didn't know I was searching for!
Anne

One performer, Robin, described the original disparate group of performers, all from opposing sides of the conflict, as initially being like the resistant poles of two magnets.

It took the Theatre of Witness process to allow us to re-orient our polarity into something connective and attractive.
Robin

Other performers describe the extraordinary connections they've built with each other in sharing their journey of creating and performing together.

I've found my true tribe! These people are my family, support network, more than friends
Anne

The love and the energy that was in the room was magical. I saw it in the looks of people when I told my story, not knowing if anyone was going to believe me. My inner spirit was flying, and the small girl in me was jumping for joy saying, "This is it, I'm free at last".
Therese

I have the strong feeling that we can make a difference. It's a feeling of excitement and expectation on the journey that we have all subconsciously agreed to make.
William

How Theatre of Witness Came to Northern Ireland

In 2009, Pauline Ross, the Founder and Director of The Playhouse in Derry-Londonderry at the time invited me to introduce Theatre of Witness to Northern Ireland. She had seen a film of *Beyond the Walls*, one of my productions, in Philadelphia. It was performed by mothers of children who had been murdered, mothers whose children were in prison, and by former prisoners. This powerful project brought these victims, parents and former perpetrators together in a community of love and compassion.

My colleague from Swarthmore College who showed the film to Pauline, explained to her about this unique form of testimonial theatre, and told her about me. It spurred Pauline's imagination, and she suggested that maybe people in Northern Ireland were finally ready to hear some of each other's true stories from the various sides of the conflict.

So Pauline invited me to Derry-Londonderry, and in one five-week visit, I interviewed over thirty-five people. I was amazed and deeply moved by the honesty and openness they all displayed: ex-paramilitaries, former security forces, victims and children of the next generation. Their stories were haunting and deeply important. I knew if I had the opportunity, I would come back. We decided to apply to the EU for a Peace III grant. When we received it, I moved to Northern Ireland, never realising I would end up staying for almost five years. But this work had become the opportunity of a lifetime.

With great vision and determination, Pauline spearheaded what turned out to be a massive project that resulted in four original productions and films, all funded by the EU Peace monies.

The first three were a trilogy focused on survivors of the

Troubles. *We Carried Your Secrets* (2009) - voices of fathers on the frontlines and those of the next generation. *I Once Knew a Girl* (2010) - the unheard stories of women and girls in Northern Ireland. And in 2012, *Release* - the stories of men from opposing sides during the Troubles.

Sanctuary (2013) was jointly created and performed by asylum seekers from Somalia and Zimbabwe alongside refugees in Northern Ireland who lost their homes due to the Troubles.

These four productions were seen by thousands of people in theatres, on film and on television. Excerpts of the films are now being viewed in workshops and presentations in schools, universities, community centres and for international audiences.

Creating and Using this Book

This book has been written in collaboration with the ten performers out of the original thirty who are still active in presenting peacebuilding workshops in Northern Ireland with The Playhouse. A chapter is dedicated to each, beginning with their scripted words from their productions, followed by their thoughts and recollections about how the process has affected them, and finally, how they see themselves as peacemakers – the Ripple Effect.

I have added my own memories, observations and reflections about the impact of their work and my understanding of Theatre of Witness as a healing modality for peace.

Quotes from the performers are written in *italics* and phrases of theirs that I view as teachings are highlighted in ***bold italics***. Central to the tenets of Theatre of Witness is that the performers are experts in their own lives and have much to teach us about the universality of resilience and transformation. As we readers bear witness to these stories, there is much that speaks to a common humanity. The insights and narratives can be used by readers for reflection and discussion about their own lives.

In addition to these chapters, the addendum includes: The Thirteen Theatre of Witness Guiding Principles, a chapter about trauma and Theatre of Witness written by Dr Thomas Spiers, and a glossary of terms.

I am so glad that the performers and I embarked together on our latest project – this book. While immersing myself once more in their stories thirteen years on, I realised their scripted testimonies form important historical documents. They describe a particular time in Northern Ireland when ordinary people were deeply hurt by the effects of the Troubles. The scripted narratives, together with their accompanying stories, describe some of the messy truth about how individuals from different backgrounds grappled with forging peace in their own lives.

The generations who have followed those who were caught up in the Troubles also live with the ripple effects, but don't always know the details. These stories offer, not only context to the actual conflict, but also understanding of how this first post-Troubles generation has figured out how to build bridges. And why those bridges are so important. These 'teachers' or 'leaders' have much to offer those who have come after them, as well as communities from other countries trying to build peace.

When we created the Theatre of Witness productions and subsequent films, I never expected that I would want to share the performers' stories in book or print form. The original live theatre productions offered audiences a place and time to gather together to bear witness and feel the emotional and spiritual effects of these stories communally. Performances were almost a ritual catharsis. One audience member described the effect of seeing *We Carried Your Secrets* as "Open heart surgery on the city of Derry". Music, film, light, gesture and true stories performed by the storytellers themselves immersed audiences in a unified experience. Why would I want to reduce all this to printed words on a page?

But time has passed, and though the live theatre performances have faded away, the ripples of the entire experience still reverberate. The performers have grown older and gained new perspective. While it was still possible, it felt essential to capture the wisdom they acquired at the time, and how it has developed in the years since, in their own voices. Someday, when we are all long gone, hopefully these words will reach open and curious souls from another generation, and the ripple effects will continue.

We, the performers and myself, aspire that this book will be used to foster ideas and inspiration.

Readers who will most benefit are:

- Those involved in peace and reconciliation
- Those who study post conflict societies
- Theatre practitioners who are interested in the methodology of Theatre of Witness
- Anyone interested in the history of Northern Ireland
- Students of leadership
- People who love stories of transformation and possibility
- Next generations in Northern Ireland who may not have known these true testaments from the conflict
- Family members of the performers
- All who have given up hope that reconciliation between people of conflicting ideologies is possible
- Artists working for social change

- Spiritual seekers

Thank you for diving into these stories. We hope they inspire you and plant seeds that will guide you in your own journey of peacemaking, whatever its shape and scope.

Teya Sepinuck, Founder and Artistic Director, Theatre of Witness, January 2023.

They say that it takes seven generations
for trauma to heal.
What will our legacy be to our
great-great-great-great-great-grandchildren?

From *We Carried Your Secrets*

Prelude

This book began when **Theresa McCann**, growing up on the Falls Road in Belfast, experienced abuse and sectarian violence that rendered her silent.

It began when five-year-old **Fionnbharr Ó HÁgain's** father, a Sinn Fein councillor, was assassinated in broad daylight and there was never any justice.

It began when **Jon McCourt** witnessed thirteen people killed by British Soldiers during Bloody Sunday.

It began when **Anne Walker,** whose uncle was killed on Bloody Sunday was later recruited as a teenager to join the IRA.

It began too when the IRA kidnapped and blew up **Kathleen Gillespie's** husband Patsy at Coshquin.

This book began when bombs exploded at Coshquin and Omagh, and police officer **Robin Young** cleaned up human body remains.

And it began when a bomb went off in Omagh, and young **Victoria Geelan** waited to see if her father, working as a police officer in the centre of the town, would return home safely.

This book also began when **James Greer's** friend was injured while they were building a bomb together as part of their involvement in a loyalist paramilitary organisation.

It began when **Syd Trotter's** activities as part of a loyalist paramilitary group led him to serve five and half years at the Long Kesh prison.

And it began when **William McKee** a Governor in HMP Maze also known as Long Kesh prison was forced to move home three times after death threats by three different paramilitary groups.

This book began too in 2009 when I moved to Northern Ireland, and together with these and nine other brave survivors of the Troubles: Catholics, Protestants, republicans and loyalists, we created, performed and toured three Theatre of Witness productions and films based on their interlocking true-life stories. These stories came from all sides of the conflict, from victims, ex-combatants, witnesses, and members of the security forces.

Above all, this book began when these 'ordinary' people shared their own life experiences of trauma, courage, regret, and transformation. Ordinary people willing to be on the frontlines of the complex process of true peacebuilding, publicly, vulnerably, and whole-heartedly.

And, when thousands of audience members rose to their feet in tears and gratitude for the courage, truth and hope displayed by these performers, that was a beginning too.

This book also began over the last thirteen years, when the performers continued to deepen their relationships with each other as they delivered national and international peacebuilding workshops in schools, community centres and theatres with The Playhouse.

And this book began again now, thirteen years later, when we decided to write these words.

We Carried Your Secrets

Fathers on the Frontlines and the Next Generation

Created and Performed in 2009

Fionnbharr
Robin
Victoria
James
Jon

There Never Was a Beginning, Middle or End

Fionnbharr Ó HÁgain

The sixteenth of September 1991.
I am five years old and at school.
It is twenty past nine in the morning. Broad daylight.
Miles away, on a busy college campus, a college instructor
opens his car door, and another man mingles with the crowd.
He wears no mask to cover his face.
He moves just twelve inches away and calls out "Bernard!"
Then he fires eight bullets from a .22
before fading back into the crowd.
My Da is done.

I remember things happening,
but I don't remember what happened when.
I was in P2. Ma came to the door of the class
and said I could take one book.
I took The Big Red Ball. Then we went and got my brother.
My sister had already been picked up before.
We were brought back to the house, brought in front of the TV.
A priest was there, uncles, neighbours.
They told us that Da was dead.
The only reason I had any idea what that meant was
that one wee lad in my class had died.

We were bundled off to Granny's house for a few days.
Brought back and forward during the wake.
Now that I think about it, that was the first time I remember
being in the house without the shutters being pulled.

I remember being lifted to say goodbye. But being too scared.
I insisted on wearing my school uniform to the funeral.
After that, we were taken to the counsellor in Belfast.

Sometimes we would go to the Jacksons'.
I remember being in their yard one day.
A patrol went past. We all got excited – guns!
The front door opened and we were told:
"Get away and stay away, 'cos they shot your Da!"
I don't remember a lot of details.
A lot I literally found out about this year.

He was on his way to work in the morning.
But he told my uncle after football,
that he knew he was being followed every day.
The UFF claimed my dad's murder.
He was shot with a .22 pistol.
It was found in a car the following February,
but the man was never arrested.
No one's ever been arrested or questioned for it.

Police had photo kits.
One was given by the woman in the bus
next to the car my Da was shot at.
It was never shown to the public.
Two witness statements were taken.
A third one - the guy says he was willing to come forward
and give his again, 'cos at the barracks,
the police tried to 'politely' talk him out of it.

His statement isn't even on the record.
None of the descriptions were shown outside of the barracks.
And the ombudsman told us that
there may not even be an investigation file.
It doesn't make me feel any better about cops.

My Ma kept a diary about how we handled it.
I don't remember much.
My brother would sit and talk to Da
as if he was still there at the dinner table.

My anger is at the man who shot me Da.
But at the end of the day, he was only following orders.
He was given orders.
I don't know how far up it went.
But someone could have stopped it.

If the man who killed my Da asked for forgiveness, I'd go mental.
I don't know whether I could stand there.
I'd have to go, otherwise I'd end up doing damage
to myself or someone else.
It would be the trigger for the ultimate bender of doom.

I'd like to see him do time at least. Some form of justice.
It would make it a hell of a lot easier.
But it would never make up for the fact
that I never got to know him.
But at least it would show that someone else cared enough
to do something about it. Something we never had.

I've never dealt with the whole thing.
Our whole family was put in counselling.
But it made me more angry.
I felt like they were trying tell me what to feel.

*When I turned eighteen, I got a letter from the Court Funds Office
saying there was £4,500 grand in compensation waiting for me.
Two grand was interest.
To me that was blood money.
I went out drinking with my mates.
I'd drink up to a litre of vodka a day.
Ended up drinking through the compensation funds.*

I had a death wish.

*I was given an ultimatum:
drink, or keep my girlfriend and band.
It wasn't really a choice.
Drinking's good craic 'cos of the music and the people.
People and music aren't good craic 'cos of the drinking.*

*I've been approached to become 'involved'.
There are still people who want me to get involved very actively,
but I can't be part of something that I don't agree with.
I'm not registered to vote because I have nothing to vote for.*

*I have a lot of anger.
It's easier to take it out on something that has nothing to do with it.
That's why I play drums.
It's the only thing I can hit and get away with it.*

*I sit down behind a kit and lose track of myself. I sit there for hours.
Music is my only escape.
I'm stuck being Bernard's son for the rest of my life.
But music, that's me. It's the only way
I'll be able to escape from this society.*

I don't want to forget about it, just not be trapped by it.
There is no beginning, middle or end. It's never had an end.

*I've always wondered why my Da got done rather than others
who were involved in the IRA with shootings and bombings.*

I just wish I could have him back.
I wish I could tell the difference between a story and a memory.
I wish that one person would get pulled to do time.
I wish that someone else had to pay for it instead of just us.

Children of the Troubles

Fionnbharr melted my heart the first day I met him. Sitting with his eyes glued to the floor, his feet tapping incessantly, his pain was visible in every imaginable way. And yet so was his strength, openness and vulnerability. He was someone I wanted to put my arms around.

Before coming to Northern Ireland, I hadn't imagined the lifelong repercussions of a father's murder on his then five-year-old son. I thought that the most potent stories of the Troubles would primarily be those of adults who had been on the frontlines. I hadn't yet understood the huge impact the conflict had on the children growing up in it.

But I hadn't met Fionnbharr.

Like many others of his generation, he fell into substance abuse and depression. But what set him apart from others was that he never got involved in sectarian violence or antisocial behaviour. Most striking, though, was that he never masked his grief through a tough exterior. Instead, his great vulnerability shone through his silence, tears and drumming. Fionnbharr used words sparingly, but his loud, fierce drumming expressed the magnitude of his pain and rage. Hitting the drums relieved some of the pressure on him to exact revenge for his father's murder. His body spoke volumes and expressed what could not be spoken.

Tears of Communal Grief

Fionnbharr cried onstage during every performance. We had filmed him narrating his part, because we knew he was too raw to speak live in front of an audience. The film was displayed on a large screen behind him while he sat onstage behind his drum kit. He played the drums before and after the film, tears running down his face.

He also cried when he spoke live on stage, representing an anonymous woman who had lost her son. Her words mirrored Fionnbharr's own feelings about his father, which allowed him to express his anguish when portraying her.

> She sits and waits at the table.
> Her hands, smoothing the tablecloth.
> No one's heard from him for over fourteen years.
> She knows in her head that he was done by one of his own.
> But her heart isn't ready to believe.
> She wants justice.
> She wants answers.
> She wants once more to hear his voice.
> But no one says anything.
> No one gives anything away.
> She sits and waits for her disappeared son.

Fionnbharr sobbed as he spoke her words, embodying her sorrow, grief and silent waiting. Her grief mirrored his own grief and sorrow. He expressed it so deeply that it became ours as well.

Two counsellors and I watched carefully before and after every show to discern how Fionnbharr was doing emotionally. Usually, he'd come offstage still in tears, but when I'd ask if it was too much for him, he always wanted to continue. We trusted his own agency and assessment that the process was healing for him. I believe that his release of tears was not just for himself, but for all people grieving in Northern Ireland. He became a conduit that allowed us to experience a communal catharsis.

Commitment

The whole process of creating and performing ToW was extraordinarily difficult for Fionnbharr. He had never expected to be involved with loyalists and police, and this project tested him to his limits.

> *If I had known at the beginning that there would be a UDA (James) and a peeler (Robin), in the project, I wouldn't have done it. When I realised, my first reaction was: F this! My Da wouldn't cow down to you. I never thought I'd call a loyalist or peeler (police) my friend.*

When we began, Fionnbharr often kept his head and eyes to the floor, not looking up at people or props that triggered him. But he came to every rehearsal and committed himself in every way possible. I recently asked him what made him commit to something that brought such strong and painful emotions to the fore.

> **You were all invested in me.**
>
> *My own stubbornness made me start. I thought I'd stick two fingers to the UDA and peelers. "I'm not walking away from you!" When I first met Teya, I didn't understand what she meant when she was explaining the project. We were already way in it when I realised I was going to have to sit with a peeler and UDA. I didn't think it would ever work. But whatever spell Teya cast on us, it fucking worked.*
>
> *I kept coming. It didn't matter how I felt. I would be shafting people if I quit. You were all invested in me. And I was invested. I never really saw it as being about me.*

> *I know that I said it was the best form of counselling, but that's not what I was doing it for. It didn't feel like counselling. I never thought of it as about me, or for me.*

Relationships and Embodiment

One of the most pivotal moments of transformation occurred early on, during a cast retreat. Fionnbharr shared his story about the murder of his father and the suspected collusion by the police and the UFF, a loyalist paramilitary organisation. He then spoke about his intense hatred of police.

Robin, then a serving police officer, listened attentively, and seemed to quietly reflect as Fionnbharr spoke. Then he gently shared how ashamed he was and offered a heartfelt apology for what the police had done. "That never should have happened." He asked if he could shake Fionnbharr's hand. Fionnbharr kept his head down and was unable to look Robin in the eye. But as Robin walked towards him with his hand extended, Fionnbharr rose, took his hand, and then pulled him into a tight bear hug. There were many tears.

In true Fionnbharr fashion, there were no words that followed the hug. It stood on its own as a moment of truth and connection. Later, his friendship with Robin grew, culminating in an opening night prank they played on me. None of it changed Fionnbharr's feelings about police in general, but he was willing to see the possibility that all police aren't the same. This felt like a solid first step towards peacebuilding, as well as a demonstration of emotional bravery from both of them.

> *I know Robin was a peeler, but I never knew him as a peeler. We're fuckin' mates. I like his honesty. He doesn't spout bullshit about a few bad apples. He knows what the organisation he worked for did. He eventually stood up. I was raging and he said he was ashamed.*

That moment of courage was one of many that Fionnbharr displayed throughout the entire process. He later told me that he was terrified before every rehearsal and performance and he's still terrified now, fourteen years later, ahead of every workshop. But he has never once let that fear prevent him from participating fully and openly.

Embodying the Enemy

When we were creating *We Carried Your Secrets*, we took scheduled rehearsal breaks. Fionnbharr, James and Jon always stood together outside, rolling papers, smoking, and taking all the time in the world. It didn't take long for conversation and laughter to flow. Fionnbharr likened it to being in a beer yard where the craic was great. Their connections organically flourished, as did their mutual respect for one another.

One day when we were rehearsing James' part, it became clear that he was better at narrating his story from a stationary position rather than simultaneously moving about the stage. Without much forethought, I looked at Fionnbharr and asked if he would step in to physicalise the younger James while James spoke. Even though Theatre of Witness is never performed by actors; in some cases, I have cast members step into scenes to amplify the story of another performer. Given that this work is also about modelling empathy and community, sometimes this creative solution adds a profoundly moving dimension to someone's story.

Fionnbharr portrayed James' life as if it were his own. He physicalised James' journey from being a disenfranchised Protestant teen, up until being released from prison. He poignantly showed us James' utter terror of being murdered by both loyalists and republicans after he was released.

> *It was 1976, the Troubles were roaring bad.*
> *There had been a lot of drive-by shootings*

> *and I was always on guard,*
> *afraid that the IRA would shoot me and*
> *afraid that the UDA would take me out.*
> **James, from We Carried Your Secrets**

Surprisingly, Fionnbharr's rage at those affiliated with the UDA did not seem to affect his willingness to portray James onstage. Instead, he let himself become James. Where words fail or seem too limited, Fionnbharr is kinaesthetically eloquent, and embodiment comes naturally. It is through his body that he most expresses his bravery and empathy, even for someone he first perceived as an enemy.

> *It's really easy to hate somebody when you don't have to look at them. It's more work to hate them when you have to look at them. Listening to James at one stage, I realise that I was on the verge of going down the same path myself from the other side. It's as simple as having been born a couple of miles up the road. The UDA and Provo men are basically all the same.*

Fionnbharr conveyed more through those silent and still moments than words could ever have expressed. He transmitted the depth of James' experience flawlessly.

In what became an iconic image deeply imprinted in my mind, Fionnbharr leaned against a folded table in absolute stillness on a darkened stage. The bright light of a flashlight, meant to imply the barrel of a gun, shone directly into his eyes. As he waited for the trigger to be pulled, Fionnbharr's eyes simultaneously conveyed both daring and utter terror. He didn't move a muscle or blink. Time stood still while haunting music amplified the tension.

When I originally asked Fionnbharr to portray James, I didn't do it as a conscious method of peacebuilding. I wasn't asking him to 'become the enemy' as a way for him to gain empathy for someone on the other side. But somehow, years later, I realised the magnitude of what I had actually asked of him.

It was a testament to his trust in the process and his willingness to be so vulnerable that allowed him to step in so full-heartedly. And once he got inside the emotional life of James, it became impossible to for him to view James as the enemy.

Embodying the Fallen

I was never far away from tears.

Perhaps the most iconic image in the production was during the Bloody Sunday scene in Jon's part. Some called it 'the Pieta moment'. In it, Fionnbharr embodied a young man who had just been killed by British soldiers. Kieran, a silent member of the cast, tenderly scooped him up and held him in his arms like Mary cradling her crucified son. With his head falling back, limbs completely limp, Fionnbharr surrendered his weight and gave himself wholly to Kieran's love and grief.

That poignant image was created by Kieran and Fionnbharr from an improvisation. I had asked the cast to explore ways of falling and then carrying each other. But I had never imagined the scene that the two of them would create. Each committed so fully to the moment, that I think it surprised even Kieran. He told me that once during a performance, that he was so moved by the grief, love and tenderness he felt towards Fionnbharr in his arms, he almost forgot they were onstage in front of an audience. He instinctively pulled Fionnbharr to his lips and almost kissed his forehead before stopping himself.

> *There was massive trust on Fionnbharr's part. It was like he was saying, "I'm ready to put my life and brokenness on your back". It was almost a spiritual moment.*
> *It was so emotional. Mary holding Jesus. Kieran had that quiet presence. A presence of the sort of guy I want to walk with. I think it displayed humanity beyond boundaries.*
> Jon McCourt

When I recently asked Fionnbharr what it had felt like being in Kieran's arms, he couldn't find any words. He only remembers the felt experience. *"I was never far away from tears".*

Liminal Time

There is no beginning, middle or end.
It never had an end.

When Fionnbharr speaks these words during his part, he is referring to the story of his father's murder and subsequent lack of investigations. But I like to think that he has also invited us to enter the time and space continuum where stories have no fixed beginnings or end. Waiting can go on forever. Events occur simultaneously. One ending can be another beginning. Opposites are held with equal measure. And time and space are liminal. It's bardo time.

That heightened sense of timelessness is often engendered in theatre, dance or music when a performer allows themself to inhabit the terrain of deep emotion, stillness and presence, and spirit takes over. Ego and self-consciousness disappear. Fionnbharr has that innate gift. It's a gift he shares with priests and shamans. It takes a certain concentrated energy. Passion. Willingness to surrender.

Time Passing

Like the anonymous mother of the disappeared son, Fionnbharr still waits. He waits for justice. He waits for answers, and he waits for the endless investigations to conclude with truth and accountability. But now, almost thirty years later, there is less and less hope for any State answers. And now he is wondering what he is passing on to his own son who will be five when Fionnbharr turns thirty-eight. The same ages he and his own father were when the tragedy struck.

> *I'm praying that my son doesn't take on the fight*
> *I've taken on.*

When I ask Fionnbharr now about his future, he expresses his fear that he won't live past his own thirty eighth year.

> *I have developed a fear complex about turning thirty-eight.*
> *I was five when my Da was murdered at age thirty-eight.*
> *My son will be five when I'm thirty-eight.*
> *I have a wish for my son.*
> *No, it's a wish for me.*
> *To be there.*

Fionnbharr has continued to fight for justice. He has also remained involved in peacebuilding workshops thirteen years after he began. I asked him if he sees himself as a peacemaker.

> *I'm more willing to hear somebody out now. I'm a bit more accepting. I can accept that somebody would join the UDA as quickly as the Provos. When you hear somebody out, you can understand what they went through to get to where they think.*

> *I don't think peace is just around the corner. I don't think it will come without a wee bit more kerfuffle. The last blood hasn't been drawn. I don't think of myself in the overall picture of building peace. But I don't think that I'm part of the problem.*

> *Theatre of Witness is a heck of a lot more complex than drumming. But I've been able to do events that I wouldn't have dared.*

There is No end

I think Fionnbharr would describe himself as a work in progress. The murder of his father touched the very core of him, and he has lived with that trauma and its effects his whole life. He is still in pain, still drinks to numb his feelings, and still continues to harbour rage. I asked him one day what the lyrics would be for a song that would express who he is. And he came up with:

> *Black, brown, and red – Guinness, rum, and rage.*

But luckily that rage has a safe and powerful creative outlet. Fionnbharr's drumming career has continued to flourish and he now teaches hundreds of young people in schools and community centres. He's a devoted father and husband and has become friends with loyalists, police, and other Theatre of Witness practitioners whom he never could have imagined being part of his life before.

While Fionnbharr may be reluctant to claim the word 'peacemaker', the fact that he still shows up for Theatre of Witness with his authenticity, grief and vulnerability intact, demonstrates a profound commitment to finding a new way forward. He may only be willing to claim that he isn't part of the problem, but his dedication and openness belie the great impact he has had in moving others towards a path of peace.

> *I am so privileged to have been able to be a part of the audience for this show - I came, thinking that I did not have any story of the Troubles for myself, and spent most of the night in tears as all the random memories came to the surface that I never thought were any part of this story. I cried during the drumming. It was the saddest part of the whole evening for me. It was beautiful. I'll be thinking now about the difference between a story and a memory.*
> **Audience member**

Fionnbharr's story may have no end. He is keeping the memory of his father's death alive and yet the story evolves through time. And that messy complexity may be the gift.

> *I do Theatre of Witness workshops now 'cos it's specifically about this horrible messy truth of it all. There's no sense to just hear one side. You need to know it all. It isn't all so clearcut and far away.*
>
> **Someone said about me that I have no back doors.**

The Dance
of Peace

Robin Young

I am Robin Young. The reason I'm not here with you in person,
is that I'm a serving police officer,
and for some people, this uniform can become the cause for attack.

Anyone who associates with me therefore takes a risk,
and although I don't mind taking that risk for myself,
I am not willing to do so on your behalf.

So today you will hear my words and see my story on film,
about going from peacekeeper to peacemaker.

I came from a Protestant loyalist background,
and although I didn't take on the political beliefs,
from early childhood, I wanted to be a soldier.
I was fascinated with military history
and the study of conflict and war.

I was a risk taker, a mountain climber
and someone who loved adventure.
As soon as I could, I joined the Ulster Defence Regiment part-time.
And then in 1986, the RUC (Royal Ulster Constabulary).

But we were a country at civil war.
I was often called on riot or anti-terror patrol,
holding back the lines.
We were stuck in the middle
trying to win something that

no one could, and no one ever did.
I saw things I didn't believe in.
I participated in things I now regret,
and I didn't do things I now wish I had.
Duplicity and complicity. We all played our parts.

I have to account for my own role. I was part of a big mechanism.
Performing my duty cost me my marriage
and damn near cost me my sanity.
Now I call it my Road to Damascus.

The 1980s. It was at the height of violence.
We'd lost nine colleagues in Newry in one go.
Explosions were so common that I got to the stage of
laying all my gear out beside my bed.
4am.
"Get your arse down here, there's been a major incident!
A bomb at a checkpoint!"
They had kidnapped Patsy Gillespie,
chained him to his van with a bomb loaded into the back,
drove to the checkpoint, and then pressed the button.

There was a huge explosion that vapourised everything.
This massive, reinforced building was blown to bits.
To make it worse, one of our guys in the observation lookout
thought that the building was under fire
and shot at his own foot patrol.
It was mass murder.
The police had no way to deal with it:
"Everybody, start clearing. Whatever you find,
document it and put it in a bag."

I started from 300 yards away and slowly moved in.
We fanned out in a circle, each taking a triangular-shaped wedge
in towards the middle of the huge crater.

The place was littered with human body parts.
I found someone's backside in a field.
No front, just the cheeks.
Into the bag.
I worked my way into the middle of the scene. Pick it up, drop it
into the bag.
There was a brick in a pile of rubble. I lifted it.
Underneath was a human heart.
Pick it up, drop it in the bag.
Pick it up, drop it in.
Up, in, up, in.

At the time of the blast, there had been seven soldiers
in the armoured personnel carrier.
I didn't want to look at what remained.
I opened the back.
Nothing.
Not one shred of anything.
The force of the blast had sucked seven human beings
out through the viewing windows, each the size of a mail slot.
Totally vapourised everything.

Being professional, you learn to flip the switch. I had a job to do.
Nine times out of ten, with the plasticity of youth,
you can get over it.
But this was the beginning of a whole new dimension.
We had no preparation.
We didn't know how to process any of what we'd witnessed.

We had to account for everything:
documents, body parts, ammunition.
I knelt down reading a document and didn't notice
that the press was surrounding us.
They knew the rule never to show a police officer's face.

So there in Derry Journal's front page was a picture of the carnage

with a little figure crouched down in the road
sorting through paperwork.
One little figure amidst all the horror.
That little figure is me, so it is.
You can keep pouring cups of water into a bucket,
but eventually the bucket will be full,
and the water will spill and leak out the sides.

In 1995, the RUC decided that we needed some type of capacity
to deal with mass disaster.
I applied for a specialist team.
I had rescue experience, and I thought that if I became well-trained,
I could be of more use.
Not just to the investigations,
but to the people who really count - families.
As our boss once said,
"I want this to be the best-trained team that was never used".

But then the call came in for Omagh.
A huge bomb in a busy Saturday street, in a wee town
most of the world had never heard of.
I was off. It was my son Christopher's birthday.
I got the call and had to just get up and go.
There is no way to describe the horror:
babies,
foreigner visitors,
a pregnant mother,
young men and women,
an officer's child…
all snuffed out in the most grotesque ways.
Endless clearing up, two weeks of body identification,
trying to ID the dead
and make them presentable to their loved ones.

That second night, as we left,
a group of people had gathered in the park

for a spontaneous prayer service.
They applauded as police walked by.
I wanted to scream,
"Why are you clapping for us?
We didn't fix anything.
We can't bring anyone back from the dead!"

After that first shift, I called home.
"Please, let me talk to Christopher.
I just need to hear his voice."
My wife didn't understand. How could she?
There was no way to translate
the horror of what I was experiencing.
As the weeks went on, I would drive back home to sleep in my bed,
even if it was only for four hours.
After zipping bodies in bags all day,
I didn't want to sit in the barracks and zip myself in.
But at home, I totally shut down.

I spent two years not talking.
I didn't get aggressive or angry, but I was the man in the anorak.
I couldn't sleep.

Every morning at three am I'd awaken.
Am I asleep or dreaming?
My eyes are open, but I can't move.
I see a baby crawling on the ceiling.
But the baby has the face of one of the Omagh dead.
I'd get up and run a triathlon every day.
I wanted to take my own life.
I didn't see my marriage falling apart.
I didn't see my sanity slipping away.
My ex-wife says that I went to Omagh one man
but came back another.

Two years down the line,
as I began slipping into depression and traumatic stress,
I was still trying to keep going.
But some of the other guys who kept going,
were going down to the bars.
Others resigned.
Some tried putting guns to their heads.
Still others drove off roads.
We lost more to suicide.
We wouldn't dream to tell people what was going on in our heads.
I refused to consume alcohol. I was scared to.
I had to hold on to whatever sanity I had left.
But one day I slipped in the kitchen,
and the glass I was holding broke.
I burst into tears.
I can't even get that right. Can't even hold a glass?
The bucket was now full.

The counsellors called it 'Post Traumatic Stress Disorder'.
A nice professional name for 'Hell'.
I was an ex-combatant, shell-shocked and in need of care.
Without Rapid Eye Movement sleep,
my mind couldn't file all the images it had seen.
Instead, scenes were logjammed in my brain, playing themselves
over and over.
I could forget nothing.
That switch was stuck in the on position and
I couldn't turn anything off.
So, we reprocessed my eye movements
and taught my brain new ways to file.
I went on desk duty and took time to heal.

Heal yes, but forget no.

My ex-wife was right. I am no longer the same man.
I am a better one.

My memories of cleaning up after so much carnage changed me.
Omagh earned me the right to speak.
I've lived through the horror of seeing what human beings
can do to each other,
and I now believe that we all have our part to play
to turn this around for our children.

I will sit down and talk with anyone, if they will try to fix this:
enemies,
combatants,
students,
elders,
members of the military.
I will listen, and I will learn, and I am willing to do anything,
provided it doesn't involve the killing of another human being
in the name of politics.
We have to stop killing our kids.
I am committed to peacebuilding, so those who died in Omagh,
Coshquin, and the rest of Northern Ireland, didn't die in vain.

Motivation

These words of Robin are testament to his motivation to take part in our first Theatre of Witness production in Northern Ireland. Like all the participants, Robin came to our work with much to gain, but also much to lose.

As the debut Theatre of Witness performance here, nobody knew how it would be received or what the pushback would be. But given that there were active death threats against police at that time, it was particularly dangerous for Robin to tell his story publicly. The locations and times of our performance tour throughout the North and over the border were widely advertised. Someone intent on making a surprise attack on him would put everyone in harm's way. His security and the security of all of us were at stake.

We therefore decided together to have Robin perform his part on film rather than appear live. And we shifted our rehearsal venues and times, to prevent any potential threats. But I think Robin knew that even those measures wouldn't necessarily protect him from becoming a target for any paramilitary group who hated police. His participation was a further example of the innate courage that is central to who he is.

Even though Robin didn't need to come to all the rehearsals, because his part was going to be on film, he was there for every one. He shared equally in all aspects of the creative process, including making suggestions in Jon's part about how the performers could more realistically portray republican rioters fighting against the police and soldiers. He even surprised us by showing up incognito to watch some of the performances and offer his support. He was an integral part of the Theatre of Witness family.

Accountability

From my first meeting with Robin, the pride he shared about his military and police service was apparent. Even his upright and centred posture indicated a man of dignified strength and self-respect, but also someone who genuinely wanted to be of service. Yet Robin was very quick to talk about how 'duplicity and complicity' played a role in his profession, and how he had done things he wished he hadn't. It was a huge admission for someone who was still currently in his position. This is what he recently wrote about those days:

> *I was never a dancer, but I was taught to dance to their tune*
> *Hands out of your pockets.*
> *Stand up straight.*
>
> *Discipline.*
> *Obedience.*
> *Do the same as everyone else.*

Cordon! Form a straight line!
Eyes front!
Shields up! Visors down!
Show batons! Load batons!
Go!

Don't ask questions. Don't argue. Don't think. Don't ever speak your mind
Do as you're told.
Just listen to us.

The first time Robin openly took a stance of accountability was early on, in relation to the suspected police collusion in the assassination of Fionnbharr's father. Fionnbharr was still so traumatised by both loyalists and police, that when Robin shared his story and showed his police uniform for the first time in our group, Fionnbharr kept his eyes closed and lowered. His foot was erratically tapping the floor.

When I asked him how he was doing, he responded, *"That's what we have eyelids for"*. I couldn't imagine how the two of them would connect, although as always, I trusted the process, and Robin was patient.

A few weeks later, the group went on a residential to a beautiful retreat centre by the sea. There, Fionnbharr told his own story about the profound effect his father's assassination had on him as a child of five. He spoke with great emotion, not holding back the expression of his hatred for the UDA and the police, who hadn't wanted to or even bothered to investigate his father's murder.

Robin listened deeply. Then he apologised to Fionnbharr on behalf of the police. *"That never should have happened."* He admitted he was ashamed to be part of the organisation that had been responsible. And, with great humility, he added: *"After one rehearsal, you were waiting outside, and I passed you, and we shook hands. That was very significant for me. If you're willing, I'd like to shake hands with you again."*

Fionnbharr was silent and shaking. But when Robin walked across the circle and stood in front of him with his hand extended, Fionnbharr rose and pulled Robin close into a big, teary bear hug. It was one of the most heartfelt and heart-breaking moments I've witnessed doing this work. Robin's compassion, empathy and accountability created an opening that allowed for the possibility of a real relationship to develop – one that has contained many elements of healing for each of them.

Words spoken in the right way and in the right context may be mightier than the sword.

In all of this work, relationships organically grow over time. Trusting everyone's own process and pace, I am often surprised at what can blossom.

Many months later, on the night of our first performance, just an hour or so before curtain, Robin came to me and said that Fionnbharr had been arrested. He offered to go down to the station right then to see if he could sort it out in time. Given that there were no understudies for the performance, and we didn't have enough time to re-rehearse and figure out how to do the show without Fionnbharr, I was devastated, and out of my mind with nerves. After ten minutes of me running around the theatre uselessly bemoaning the situation, both of them appeared laughing.

It had all been a big wind-up they had been planning for a week. Robin later said it was Fionnbharr's idea. The fact that he now trusted Robin enough to suggest they play a prank on me was proof of how far their relationship had come. While a part of me wanted to scream, I also understood the significance of their shared delight at pulling off this caper.

> *Peacebuilding is like dancing the waltz.*
> *Sometimes you push and sometimes you yield.*
> *It takes two separate people, who together give and take.*
> *Sometimes it's faster and sometimes it's slower.*
> *And sometimes you don't feel like you're moving at all.*

Listening in a New Way

From the outset, Robin decided, that to be a part of this peace-making initiative, he wanted to transform his ingrained way of listening to stories.

> After the Omagh bomb I was looking for something to stop it from happening again, and if it meant listening with respect to performers like James (from a loyalist paramilitary group), and Anne (from a republican paramilitary background), then I was ready.
>
> **Instead of switching off, I need to switch on.**
>
> I need to hear narratives that I'm not comfortable with.

Years of adhering to police policy had taught him that his job was to:

> Decide who was in the right and then use lawful force to the one who was doing wrong. James and Anne were considered wrong from a policing standpoint. They were criminals. But from a peacemaker point of view, I needed to listen to their narratives. Peace-making is about listening to all sides. You might never find out who's right or wrong. I learned that I have to listen to everyone's narrative.
>
> The first time I heard James' story, I got a shock when I heard the part about him building a pipe bomb. Before that, I knew he was in the UDA, (the loyalist paramilitary Ulster Defence Association), but I liked him. I thought I liked him, but then when he told us about building the bomb, he had said something I didn't like. But then I thought to myself. What did you expect him to say? He already said he was UDA.
>
> I'm hearing things I'm not comfortable with, but now I'm at the stage where I'm learning to stay with the discomfort. I learned to relish the uncomfortable conversations. That's where peace-making lies.

Robin met Anne when he offered to support the second year's

Theatre of Witness production, *I Once Knew a Girl*, that she performed in.

> *The first time I heard Anne's story about being in the IRA, it didn't surprise me. I had known her as a suspect. Her name had been in the back of my notebook, and we had been instructed, "If you see her, get a female officer and search her". But soon after working together, she and James were no longer suspects to me. They were just James and Anne. They weren't judgmental of me, and I didn't want to be judgmental of them. They treated me with the same compassion that I tried to show them when I shared my own story.*

Hearing Anne's point of view about what it had been like to be constantly searched and harassed by police, Robin admitted that there had been times when on duty, he too had stopped and provoked people because he could. He had had the power and the uniform. But as he acknowledged:

> **Just because you have the right, it doesn't make it right.**

The above is now a precept that Robin lives by. He teaches it when working with police groups overseas who are dealing with their own prejudices and lack of accountability. He often says that the most powerful teaching tool he has is telling stories about his own mistakes. It opens a path for others to examine their own prejudices. For instance, with police in Eastern Europe, he starts by explaining:

> *"I'm not here to tell you I'm the expert who got it right all the time", I tell them. "I'm here to tell you I'm an amateur who got it wrong, so YOU can get it right more of the time."*
> *And through God's blessings of silence and speech, eventually, however reluctantly, they speak to me: "I don't know why I told that racist joke", says one. "When it was my turn to be stereotyped as corrupt, it really stung!." "I don't know why I told you they couldn't be trusted," says another. "When my own personal experience showed me they could!." "We get the*

stories you tell. They've helped change our thinking."

As another example of his own change of heart, Robin says:

Fionnbharr, James and Anne continue to change my life. Being able to listen to Anne, someone who I would have seen as the enemy, has helped me to apply that listening to others and give them the benefit of the doubt.

In order to make peace, you don't speak to friends, you speak to your enemies. One of my main values is to be willing to talk and listen to everyone.

The Need for Stories and Emotional Truth Now

It's been twenty-four years since the signing of the Northern Ireland Peace Agreement. And since that time, there have been countless Inquiries and proposals for victim compensation that have gone nowhere. Government leaders have come and gone. Along with them, countless promises of justice.

Theatre of Witness may be the only form of truth-telling we have left.

There's more need now for Theatre of Witness, especially since Northern Ireland's new legislation to end all prosecutions and inquiries related to the Troubles before 1998. With no more legal recourse, nothing else can happen to reveal the truth except a mechanism like Theatre of Witness. It may be the only form of truth-telling and inquiry left for victims. There are still people who want to draw a line under the past and say "Don't bring it up". But I believe that we have to keep bringing it up until we learn not to do it again.

Emotional truth is more valuable to people than hard cold facts.

> *Theatre of Witness and storytelling will do better than inquests and historical inquiries anyway. It means that, instead of sticking with the absolute cold hard facts, people can express their emotional truth which is more valuable. As someone who came through the Omagh Bomb inquest, it didn't help to go the legal route of just hearing someone's name and how they died. It was mechanical and emotionless and caused more hurt. No one at the inquest asked what the circumstances of someone's life and death were. That's what people mean when they say they want the truth.*

In 2009, Robin went to South Africa to study the effects of their Truth and Reconciliation Commission.

> *In South Africa, the only stories that were part of the Truth and Reconciliation Commission were the ones from people who had been perpetrators of murder or victims of torture – the apparently 'big' stories. People who were brutalised and searched daily were pushed to one side in favour of 'real stuff'. But the real stuff is what happens to people in their daily lives. Even if a story is very small, it still has the same value as a big one. The important thing is that through Theatre of Witness, someone like Victoria could voice her fear of having not having a story that 'counted' and find out that it did.*

When I was casting the net for a group of performers for We Carried Your Secrets, I originally was caught up in looking for the 'big' stories also. I thought I needed to seek only people who had been actively involved in the conflict, not people who lived the ripple effect. But it was when I met Victoria, age twenty-six and the daughter of a police officer, that I became aware how limited my vision had been.

Victoria had asked if her story counted, because no one had been killed or injured in her family. She eloquently expressed the fear she had borne every day as she searched under the car for bombs before getting in. And her belief that everyone in Northern Ireland had scars – "seen and unseen".

I learned from her that it is in fact often the hidden, more private stories that make up the fabric of a society trying to heal from the collective trauma of war. They are the legacy of what will be passed down to the next generation. Victoria was a prime example.

Victoria and Robin built a deep and lasting friendship. She felt safe enough to ask him questions about being in the police that she was afraid to ask her own father at the time. He treated her with the utmost respect, learning from her about the impact of policing on the next generation.

For many years, Robin's son Christopher lived in Wales. But when he returned to Northern Ireland as a teenager, Robin needed to teach him about the complexities of the place to ensure his safety.

> *I had to give him what I what I affectionately call 'Northern Ireland 101'. I don't know whether I could have had that conversation with Christopher if I hadn't done Theatre of Witness. One of the things I did was show him the DVD of our show, so that he had some concept of the community and what the society was now living through. And talking to Victoria gave me the courage to be absolutely and completely honest with Christopher.*

Another unintended ripple effect.

Now and Future

Robin retired from the police after thirty years. He has since become an independent consultant, helping organisations facilitate greater understanding of the issues of minority communities. As he says, he never asks anyone to do something he himself hasn't done. And he likes to teach by using his own mistakes as examples. He teaches through peacebuilding workshops organised by The Playhouse, as part of a team with the other nine performers, as well as through his own organisation.

> *Now I'm a facilitator,*
> *transforming conflicts between states*
> *and communities all over Europe.*
> *I've talked to people I wouldn't talk to.*
> *I've talked to people who wouldn't talk to me.*
> *I've talked to anyone who would listen*
> *and many who would not.*
> *Arms folded, chin out, tight lipped.*
> *Stonewalling, but I kept talking.*
>
> *I learned to dance the dance, give a little when it needed it.*
> *Push a little when the opportunity presented.*
> *A shuffle back here, a step forward there.*
> *Always moving, now leading, now being led.*
> *Regal rhumbas.*
> *Frantic foxtrots.*
> *Jittery jigs.*
>
> *And through God's blessings of silence and speech, eventually,*
> *however reluctantly,*
> *they speak to me.*
>
> *I'm teaching people to dance to the tune of tolerance.*
> *The rhythm of respect.*
> *The harmony of humanity.*
> *The concerto of compassion.*
> *The prelude to professionalism.*
>
> *Don't just do as you're told. Think it through.*
> *Don't just do the same as the rest. Think for yourself.*
> *Listen, and above all, talk to everyone.*

About his co-facilitators, Robin expresses the deep relationships of trust they have built through thirteen years of working together.

> **I have a level of trust not only for them,**
> **but also for their judgement.**

There are still staunch republican and loyalist areas of Northern Ireland, where it remains dangerous for an ex-police officer to be public. But it is exactly those places where entrenched sectarian prejudice still thrives. And where there is the most hope for the possibility of change.

Thirteen years ago, Robin never would have felt safe enough to go to some of these places to co-facilitate workshops. Just walking from his car to the venues would have been too dangerous. But now, when either Anne or James invites him, he says yes. He trusts them. He trusts them with his safety.

> *Those Theatre of Witness relationships have matured to the point where we quite literally trust each other with our lives.*

Robin, a Quaker, wants to close his chapter with a word about the role of God in his life. He calls it the thread that runs through everything. George Fox's words offer wisdom he clings to.

Walk cheerfully over the world, answering that of God in everyone.[1]

---

1. The Yearly Meeting of the Religious Society of Friends, (1995), *Quaker Faith and Practice (2nd Ed)* 19:32

What Do We Pass from One Generation to the Next?

Victoria Geelan

Let me tell you what I see
Shapes and shadows
Light and dark
Forms without faces

I see colour and shine
Mirrors and projection
Stories and questions

I've been trying to understand where I fit in
But whose eyes do I look through?

When I ask, some tell me about history, land and wars
Others, about religion, clan and tribe
Some say it's about freedom, oppression, poverty and class

Do we all hear with different histories coursing through our genes?
Different music in our ears?
Different colours in our eyes?

What do we pass from one generation to the next?

A war? The remains of a war?
The truth? A lie?
Or maybe a story, a question, a dream
Since I was a little girl, I've always had questions
I remember walking down the street and seeing the Orange Hall
"Mammy, if it's the orange hall, why is it painted blue?"
And to my father, "Daddy, what does IRA mean?
Maybe I was too young to understand any answer
I might then have asked "What's a Republican?
Am I a Republican?"
What do you tell a child?
When are you old enough to be told the truth?
When do you have a story?
When does your story count?

When I was four, my Daddy took a picture
of me wearing his RUC uniform.
When he'd come home at night, he'd take it off
and hang up his gun.

My daddy always made me feel safe.
Every time he left the house, he hugged me
like it might be the last time.
I was taught not to lie,
but we weren't supposed to tell anyone that Daddy was in the police.
Some things are too dangerous to say.
Checking under the car for bombs was a daily activity.
At night in the dark, I would get scared.
Who were the bad men who wanted to hurt my Daddy?

My father is Protestant, and my mother is Catholic.
I grew up in both worlds, trying to forge my identity
as a mixed child.
Children at school would ask, "Are you a cup or a plate?"
I identified as Catholic, so I'd say "cup".
When I was about ten, a kid told me that he knew what I was.

"Right. You're an albino."
I had never heard that word before.
It's a condition caused by a recessive gene that both parents have.
Even though my mother is Catholic and my father Protestant,
they both share that gene.
It means that I don't produce melanin and my eyesight is poor.

I see shapes and shadows,
light and dark,
forms without faces.
Technically I could register as blind, or wear special glasses to
'correct' my vision.
But why do I have to see like everyone else?
My eyesight hasn't stopped me from passing A levels
in Spanish, French and geography,
going to university or traveling around the world alone.
Metaphorically I'm blind and sighted at the same time.
Being between the two gives me access to both worlds.
I can be Protestant and Catholic, Irish and British,
sighted and blind,
a good place to be if you live in a land of conflict.
In Latin, the word albino means 'Little Dawn'.

August 1998.

I was fifteen.
The day of the bomb, my father was out on duty,
stationed ten miles away from our home in Omagh.
I was meant to go into town just a short distance away
from our house to buy some stationery,

but was still at home with my mother, sister and aunt,
when the force of the blast shook the house.
We kept waiting for my father as the death count went from eight,
to thirteen,
to twenty.
The phone lines were cut off and he had no way of reaching us.

I only just learned that the police had heard over their radios that
one of those killed was a police officer's child.
They didn't know whose.
Daddy lifted the blankets looking for us
in the makeshift morgue on the street.

I didn't know what to do.
We went to the bottom of our driveway
and watched buses taking the injured up to the hospital.
People were covered with blood-stained towels,
but I felt so far removed.
All I could see was red against white.
There were two hundred people hurt or killed.
People from Spain, Buncrana, Omagh.

When we finally found Daddy
still on duty in the town centre at 7pm,
he said we were the most beautiful sight he'd ever seen.

I learned the name of everyone who had died
and recited them to myself at night before I went to sleep.
I remember thinking there were thirty killed –
the same number as a class in my school.
I tried to imagine a whole class gone and me walking in.
No one else there.
We were given surveys within a month of starting school that asked
"Are you stressed?"
A twelve-year-old fellow in our school lost his leg.

No one talked about it. We were all supposed to just get on with it.

My father hasn't been the same since the Omagh bombing.
After I finished secondary school,
I decided to stay at home an extra year
before going to University so as not to leave him.
I thought I might be the glue that was holding him together.
He never talked about what he witnessed,

and I didn't know how to bring it up.
I didn't want to be responsible for bringing my daddy to tears.

I have so many questions. So much was downplayed,
probably to protect us.
The word 'war' was never used. It's not kitchen table conversation.
People think that because we lived through part of it,
we know the stories; we understand the emotional aftershock.
But we don't. We know bits and pieces.
It's like trying to fit the pieces of a jigsaw puzzle together
without knowing what the picture is.

I want to ask my father if he ever used his gun.
Did he witness brutality?
What's his story? What's mine?

When I compare my own life experiences with those of others,
I feel as though I have no right to feel pain.
No one in our family was killed. No one was physically injured.
Compared to so many others in Omagh, Northern Ireland,
and around the world,
I have not suffered. I have no tragic story.

But why do we compare and judge our experiences?
Why do we measure who has suffered the most?
None of us who lived through the violence here
have been left unscathed.

We all bear the scars - seen and invisible.

**I was born in the middle of the Troubles.
We've been carrying the secrets of those who came before us
since the day we were born.**

A Question

Victoria's poetic and penetrating questions were what drew me to her right from the beginning. We first met at a peace gathering, where, following the testimony given by a republican ex-combatant, Victoria raised her hand. With a clear, yet trembling voice, she spoke about the trauma she experienced being the teenage daughter of a police officer living in Omagh at the time of the bomb. She then asked the question: given that no one was injured or killed in her family, did her story count?

From her tears and anguished voice, it was apparent how deeply felt her question was. Although Victoria's question was personal, she also posed very significant universal questions. Whose pain matters most in the hierarchy of traumatic experiences of the Troubles in Northern Ireland? Who can be considered a victim? Why do people feel they have to compare suffering?

I knew that she had just given us the key to the whole project, and I asked to meet with her. I quickly discovered that Victoria has the soul of an artist. In addition to being a beautiful jazz singer, she has a poetic way with words and thoughts that somehow gets to the heart of issues. She became the linchpin in my recruiting performers.

Victoria thought that her bandmate and drummer, Fionnbharr, had a compelling and important story. His father, a Sinn Fein councillor, had been assassinated during the Troubles with the suspected aid of police collusion. During our discussions, he shared that when Victoria had first joined his band, he hadn't known her father had been in the police. He confessed that if he had known, he never would have shaken her dad's hand. But Theatre of Witness gave them a new, safe context to explore their stories and emotions about growing up with fathers who had been on the frontlines of the Troubles, albeit from opposite sides. It also was a project that would invite their creativity and artistry.

Before meeting Victoria and Fionnbharr, I hadn't realised how significant intergenerational trauma was in Northern Ireland. Listening to them guided me to the decision to create an intergenerational production. I filled out the cast with three fathers who had been on the frontlines from various sides of the conflict, and an additional young adult who had been living with the ripple effects. I brought the group together to start the real work of listening, creating community and developing a Theatre of Witness production.

Listening with the Ears of Your Heart

My first goal was to create a safe space where each member could tell their story honestly and fully without being questioned or attacked. From the beginning, everyone showed one another tremendous respect. The power of what we were trying to do – form a safe circle that included stories from all sides, was palpable. Each participant showed their own deep vulnerability, with many tears, especially Victoria.

> *Having someone listen to you is empowering.*
>
> *When we first began meeting, Teya spoke about 'Listening with the Ears of Heart'. I thought it was airy fairy then. Growing up, I had been taught that I was physically strong and that I was brave. Part of being brave was not crying when someone called me names.*
>
> *But it was a release to cry with the Theatre of Witness group. I began to see the power in being vulnerable. Yes, horrible things had happened and talking about them made me cry. But I felt the empathy when the group listened to me. And I felt empathy in hearing their stories. Now thirteen years later,*

that empathy is still there. I've put work, time, and care into those relationships. I feel really good about our work.

There was safety in the space, safety of the process. I felt cared for. I felt included. People were attentive to my needs. The key to creating that safe space is in listening and being listened to. Having someone listen to you is empowering.

My experience with Theatre of Witness was that people listened with open hearts and interest.

I used to listen to be offended. I'd think, I'm not safe. Someone's disrespecting me. They don't like me. My experience with Theatre of Witness is that people are listening with open hearts and interest. So my speaking changes, and it becomes more open, compassionate, compelling and humble.

Interpreting the World with Questions

Early on, Victoria provided us with a powerful metaphor about seeing. She started by sharing with the group how her eyesight is affected by albinism. Where most of us see clear faces and objects, she sees shapes, colours and shadows that need decoding. Rather than potentially holding her back, living with those visual limitations has actually encouraged her to question and wonder about the perspectives from which we all see.

Victoria has never allowed issues with her eyesight to keep her from expanding her vision of the world. Her knowledge of other languages and years of living and travelling abroad positioned her to see the world from a variety of perspectives; something not common for many young people in Northern Ireland. She learned to be curious.

I was quite a voracious learner at university. Not just in

> regard to books, but also what I'd ask people. "Tell me things. Tell me about your country. What have you done with your life? What is this? What does that word mean?" I was constantly excited to be around people who were excited about learning. So it was hard to come back to Northern Ireland where I found closed minds.
>
> I have always believed that the healthiest of minds is a curious mind. The healthiest way to live is to go from one question to another, and to feel the excitement from it, even if you experience a devastating truth.

Victoria's innate desire to ask penetrating questions served our group well. She wasn't afraid to ask the hard questions of others, as well as of herself. Her expansive curiosity and willingness to take big risks was a powerful model for us. She became one of the most poetic voices of our group.

> **The healthiest way to live is to go from one question to another.**

Sectarianism

Growing up in sectarian Northern Ireland with a Catholic mother and a Protestant father, Victoria lived constantly with the question of identity.

> I had absorbed so much. There I was, the daughter of a Catholic mother and a Protestant father, and I had been taught that the Irish language was synonymous with the IRA which was synonymous with terrorism.
>
> When my mother had been pregnant with me, a fellow police officer had asked my parents whether I would be a boy or girl. Another one said, "What difference does it make? When the baby comes out, it will have IRA tattooed on its feet", referring to my Catholic mother.

> *On the other side, I remember being in a conversation with someone at a bar in Derry who offered me a light. I thanked him and we exchanged names. When he heard that my name was Victoria, he said, "What? Your parents named you THAT? Your parents name you after the Famine Queen!?" It was him drawing the line in the sand, categorising, and rejecting me because of my name. I was proud of myself for diffusing the moment with humour. "No, they named me after my father's ex-girlfriend." I chose to have a good punchline rather than a good punch.*
>
> *It frustrates me how many people talk of two communities. There is only one, or there are many.*
> *Don't try to fit everyone into green or orange.*

Upon Victoria's return to Northern Ireland after living abroad, the normality of sectarianism and violence struck her deeply.

> *Because of sectarianism, I'd think:, Oh, that's not a safe place to go, or safe thing to say, or a safe thing to do. Rather than use this word, I'll use that word. And having been away for four years, feeling so free from all of that, to then come back and have to be tentative again with everything was so hard. I was trying to be the most likeable or least offensive to people. I was always aware of my identity.*
>
> *Now, I don't think my partner understands how much I'm trying to unlearn all the time. To unlearn twenty-odd years of what I know, and what I was told was the way things are, is exhausting! Things like Irish names being synonymous with Republican families and terrorism. Or that the Irish language was spoken by terrorists or terrorist sympathisers.*
>
> **I'm trying to unlearn all the time.**

Victoria and her Spanish partner have given their son an Irish name - Lorcan. It's another way of claiming that her family's identity doesn't fit into any sectarian or racial box.

Secrets

The intergenerational nature of *We Carried Your Secrets* was perhaps one of the most essential aspects of this particular production. Considering how much is often hidden or kept secret in families, it gave the younger people freedom to ask the older men questions about the Troubles they had never been able to raise with their own parents or relatives.

During a residential workshop with the cast early on, I invited the younger participants to come up with a list of questions they wanted to ask their elders. I remember the most profound was: *"What does it feel like to kill someone?"* I think we all gasped when they asked that. But rather than being offended, the men answered it with great care.

Being in *We Carried Your Secrets* gave Victoria a safe place where she could talk freely about her father being in the police for the first time in her life. Much of that safety also came from the relationship she built with Robin, who was then a serving police officer. He encouraged Victoria to ask him anything she wanted, and they spent many hours in deep conversation, often with tears. His openness and generosity allowed her to ask the questions she could not ask her father. Robin and Victoria's friendship has continued to grow over these past thirteen years.

One day, following discussion by the older performers about details of their involvement in the Troubles, Victoria turned to them and said, *"We've been carrying your secrets since the day we were born"*. I remember feeling chills up and down my arms, knowing that she had just stated something powerfully and poetically true about the intergenerational ripple effects of the conflict. In that moment I knew we had found the title of our first production.

Familial Healing

Growing up I had a lot of fear that if I said the wrong thing, it could be catastrophic.

From my father, I learned that if I said the wrong thing, bombs would explode, and people could die.

The weight of the secrets that children were expected to keep due to the conflict was considerable. And because the Troubles and its aftermath was a time when the abnormal passed as normal, there was no way to acknowledge or integrate the trauma the younger generation was living through. They were asked to keep secrets of life and death. And secrets were withheld from them that could have helped them understand what their parents were going through.

Given that Victoria grew up with the understanding that revealing a secret could cause someone's death, it's particularly significant that she was later willing to speak about so much that she had kept hidden. It required exceptional bravery and vulnerability.

But it also took courage on her father's part. Even though Victoria's father had retired from the police four years earlier, there was still the potential danger that he would be targeted as a former police officer. As in all Theatre of Witness productions, I requested that every performer vet their script with those they spoke about in their part. Victoria had shown her script to her parents. But seeing the words on a page is very different from watching your loved one say them out loud to a large audience.

I spoke the truth and it brought us closer as a family.

I gave the script to my parents and asked them if there was anything in it that they didn't want me to say. That whole process showed them how much I loved them and how much I didn't want to hurt them.

> *When we did the first performance of 'We Carried Your Secrets' and I had outed my father, I was terrified. But nobody did die. I spoke up and nobody died. I spoke the truth and it brought us closer as a family.*

While *We Carried Your Secrets* focused on fathers and young adults whose dads had been actively engaged during the Troubles, Victoria is now highly aware of the missing voice of her mother.

> *Going into this project, I saw my father as the hero. But the truth is that my mother was dealing with so much on her own. Now I can see how her quiet 'getting on with things' kept us together as a family. Becoming a mother myself, I now empathise with my mam in ways I couldn't in 2009. I am grateful for all the ways she supported me then and now.*
>
> *While I was working on 'We Carried Your Secrets', my family started talking about things. It was my way of saying, "I'm ready for you to hear me, and I'm ready to listen to very uncomfortable truths". It was far more of a coming-of-age process than university and graduation.*
>
> *Performing the show was a tremendous act of courage for everyone, as well as my parents.*

Victoria's parents came to the opening night of the performance. In the film documentary of the show, the camera focusses on Victoria and her father hugging and sobbing in each other's arms after the performance. It was a raw and honest moment of profound grief.

> *My father said afterwards that he knew the show was going to be powerful, but he hadn't expected 'that'. What really got him was Robin's part. He was in awe that Robin said what he said about his own mental health and wanting to take his own life. I was aware that all of the men were vulnerable, including my father.*
>
> *My father has always been a hugger. He was the person who gave us all physical affection. That hug we had, showed that*

> the balance in our relationship had changed. He needed the hug more than I did. I think there was survivor's guilt in that hug for both of us, as well as huge relief and grief.
>
> The lines from my part that stayed with my father were when I said, "After I finished secondary school, I decided to stay home an extra year before going to university, so as not to leave him. I thought I might be the glue that was holding him together." He hadn't known that.
>
> My father didn't feel safe expressing certain things. Through Theatre of Witness, I was able to honour him in his own lifetime.

Where Do these Stories Fit?

Theatre of Witness gave Victoria a new process through which she could sort her own memories out from those of her parents. And it gave her a vehicle to explore where she fit within the larger narrative of the conflict and its aftermath in Northern Ireland, as well as abroad.

> Going to university had already been decided for me. But I chose to participate in Theatre of Witness. It was a real sense of ownership to me.
>
> It was far easier to go to a completely foreign country when I was younger and hear them talk about their conflict and wars, than it was for me to really examine my own relationship to the conflict in Northern Ireland. Sometimes when that comes up in workshops, Robin and I both talk about the shame attached to what now is known as facts; not only about the police, but about the whole system.
>
> In doing 'We Carried Your Secrets', I was facing my own story and the wounds in my own country.
>
> We were putting our heads above the parapet. We were shaking off a whole lot of shame. I'm now able to recognise

> the shame, including the shame of having my father in the police. I didn't make the choice for my father, and now I realise that he didn't want to make that choice either. He had to support his family with very few options for employment available.
>
> I've learned from my experience with Theatre of Witness that we are all products of our circumstances.
>
> **I just want to grab the whole thing by the heart, because there is an 'effing' heart in there. I wanted to embrace everything.**

Community of Practitioners

Thirteen years after Theatre of Witness began in Northern Ireland, Victoria, now in her late thirties, lives in a blended family with her partner and their young son in Derry. She sings regularly at clubs and festivals and is raising her children with consciousness and intentions of peace.

Along with nine other performers, Victoria has continued to offer local and international peacebuilding workshops with The Playhouse. The deep Theatre of Witness process they went through has laid a path for the enduring support and trust they feel for each other. Victoria has been passionate about her ongoing involvement. So much so, that she co-facilitated a workshop when her baby son was only six days old.

> It is telling that I'm still choosing to do this work. Relationships developed were very close, and we went through a grieving experience when the live productions ended.
>
> It's the work that connects us. What better foundation to have with colleagues than an all-encompassing and life-altering process? It's not just the experience of us performing, because that was short – but it was the process. It took over many aspects of our lives and psyche.

I did a workshop one time with Fionnbharr and James. We were a Fenian, a half Jaff (the term comes from a Jaffa cake that has orange in the middle and is a pejorative term for Protestant), and an ex-UDA man. Another description of us could have been, two musicians and a social worker.

I love knowing that there is comedy as well as great beauty in us sitting in a room together. There had been trust when we did the show, but now our conversations are deeper, and we have even more trust. There is never a wasted word or moment. We don't need to do polite conversation. We get into nitty gritty or hilarity. That whole feeling of what I was doing for a long time; trying to be the most likeable, or least offensive to people, is gone.

We are an army of peaceful warriors. A band of brothers and sisters. We have a sense of family. We have kinship.

Peace Workshops

There's almost a nutritional value in this work.

In the workshop, wisdom comes from many places. Participants have insights and we hold the space the way a therapist does. We hold the space so they can explore whatever comes up for them. I couldn't do it alone. It is key that there are two other people with me. Sometimes participants get emotional after seeing the videos and there are a lot of tears. I know there is huge value if people are willing to open themselves up and listen and be present and allow themselves to feel.

Often participants don't want to leave – they want to stay for three hours instead of two. There's almost a nutritional value in it. It feeds that part of ourselves that mainstream culture doesn't. It says something about art and the commercialisation of it. It is a multi-media art form that brings up many themes. It's where art and social justice meet

Impact on Audiences

Sometimes it's less about the words than how people approach me. I was in an airport in Belfast and a woman came and tugged on my sleeve, "I saw you in Theatre of Witness". She needed to tell me. She felt safe to talk. I think about how close people felt to me after seeing my part.

I look back and remember before Theatre of Witness began, when I felt that maybe my story didn't count, because nobody had died in my family. At a recent workshop, a woman shared that she had been a police officer in the RUC in the late 90s. She was in tears because my part made her think about her own children. It gave her determination to have the conversation with her children.

Recently someone asked us if we thought of ourselves as women peacemakers? The word 'women' didn't seem necessary. But 'peacemakers', yes. That doesn't mean that I'm any kind of angel though. There is this notion of what a peacemaker is – like an archetype. Everybody has a different view in their head. But to me, it is about practicing what you preach.

What do we pass from one generation to the next?
A war? The remains of a war?
The truth? A lie?

Or maybe a story, a question, a dream.

Now more than ever, I'm committed to the healing power of the arts. My work in music and Theatre of Witness here have led me to that.

The dream is limitless.

The River

James

Prelude

It is nearing my son's seventeenth birthday.
A time I've been dreading since the day he was born.
He doesn't know that at his age I'd been in an organisation
and then jail.
Not wanting him to hear it from someone else,
I promised myself I would tell him the story when he got this age.
So he wouldn't follow in my footsteps.
I screw up my courage and bring him to the place it happened.
After I tell him, he looks at me with amazement and shock.
"Daddy, I always knew there was something."

The River

I was reared along the riverbank.
My father taught me how to read the waters.
You'd learn to watch the river and it will tell you things.

Wee ones reared by the river learn its ways.
When it rains upcountry, the water rises.
As lads, we'd put sticks in at the high-water mark,
so that later, we'd know how deep it would get.
We'd laugh at the Derry boys who would come down from the city
and get stranded on the sand beds.

We knew not to fish when the water was brown.
Better to let it run off for a day until it turned black,
then it would be good for fishing.
It was black the day Thomas drowned.

It happened over forty years ago when I was eleven.
My friends and I were crossing the river
on a plank of wood over to the island.
I turned around, and saw that a young fellow
of about seven-years-old was following us.
He walked part of the way across, but then he started to cry,
because the waves were scaring him, and he couldn't get back.
We broke off two hazel rods for him to grab hold of.
My friend Sam was in front, and I was behind.
When we got to the centre, both of them slipped off.
Luckily Sam washed onto dry ground,
but Thomas washed out to deeper water.

Living by the river, we were always told that if something happened,
go get an adult.
I ran up the bank to the road and flagged down a car.
"Help us! Help us! There's a wee boy in the river!"
A car stopped.
In the passenger seat was an old man
wearing a suit and soft hat, clutching a walking stick.
He said, "I can't help you son, I'm in my good clothes."
I said, "Right – please give me your walking stick – that will do".
He held it up against his chest, closed the car door and drove off.

I ran back where Thomas was
bobbing along through the rough rapids
into deeper water.
I held on to a branch, my friends held the other end,
and I waded in almost up to my neck.
The current started to sweep me away.
I could see that Thomas still was holding the stick and was reaching

his hand out.

His eyes were wide open.
I reached out to him, and my fingers brushed the tips of his.
Our hands touched in the cold water – so close.
His eyes were wide open, his red hair floating like seaweed.
His face was as white as a ghost…
and then he just rolled over and vanished.

He wasn't found for three days.
Life carried on as usual.
When I got home, my mother told me to go up and
take off my wet clothes.
I went back to school the next morning,
and nothing was ever discussed.
The inquest came and went.
We just went back to our lives,
fished and played as though nothing had happened.

But that day, the river claimed a wee lad named Thomas.
And I still see his white face, and wide-open eyes looking up at me
over forty years later.

I wonder if that was one of life's turning points that
changed me forever.

The Bones of a War

People who know me now, see me as a dedicated father and
grandfather,
a hard worker and peaceful man.
But during my teen years you could say
hat I fell into the wrong hands.
It's a part of my life I've tried to bury and forget.
But like thousands of ex-combatants walking the streets,
it never really goes away.

It's a bag of shame that I carry around,
like Gulliver, towing his warships behind him in the Lilliputian seas.
Even then, I knew it was wrong.
But it was just something that happened during that time.
I tell my son now,
"We were all just a part of history".

It was the height of the Troubles.
My father was talking about how "The IRA was starting up again".
I didn't know what I wanted to do with my life.
I dropped out of school at age fifteen
and started working as a joiner,
helping to build the RUC station on Strand Road.
Often we were sent home because there was so much tear gas.
But sometimes we'd sit up on the roof
and watch what was happening.
We'd see lots of explosions.
The first thing you'd see would be a huge flash of light.
Silence.
And then all kinds of things would fly through the air:
planks, glass, bricks, slate.
And then a massive, massive bang followed again by silence.
We'd watch those explosions in horror and amazement.

One day during lunch break,
I walked down to the recruiting base and
joined up with the Irish Rangers.
I don't even know what I was thinking,
except that I wasn't happy with what I was doing.
I spent a year there training in weapons,
but when they wanted to send me overseas to Cyprus,
I decided to leave.

Back home, the violence and rioting had intensified.
There were barricades everywhere.
The UDA at that time was like the Neighbourhood Watch.

A defence organisation.

*A defence organisation that needed a
continuing supply of young people.*
"We are oppressed.
If we don't stand up for ourselves, we'll be trampled into the ground.
If they're not for you - they're agin' you."
Next thing you know, someone says, "Let's join up then".

It's all very nice at the start. But it's serious, not to be taken lightly.
You have a gun in one hand and bible in the other hand and
you're told that the only way out is in a box.
It's Death or Glory.
Then you're pushed to doing small things like breaking windows.
But it graduates to more serious things
until you're in a position that you can't refuse, or they'll kill you.
You're sucked in so far, but there's no turning around.

Because I had a year military training and was good with guns,
I became a quartermaster. I took the guns here and there.
I had no idea what I was really doing.

On October 10th, 1974, we were sent out to do something
and it went wrong.
My friend and I were handling a pipe bomb, and it exploded.
The moment it happened, I heard nothing,
just a massive flash of light.
Then blood.
My friend's arm had been blown off.

The four of us were arrested. My house was raided,
and they found a lot of weapons and bomb-making documents.
We were interrogated for three days before remanded to the Crum.
I was just nineteen years old and in total culture shock.
As they say, "The novelty wears off in the first 10 minutes".
I was in prison till I was twenty-three.

If I could go back and change it all tomorrow,
I'd do it in a heartbeat.

It was scary and horrible, but at the same time it was an education.
Some of the people there were psychopaths
who would have no trouble cutting your throat.
Many's a night I slept with one eye open.
But there was also a lot of camaraderie.
I met some of the most infamous and interesting people
this country has ever known.

We ran the place.
The UDA in those days was run on the tight military model.
I was the Sergeant Major, in charge of the drill.
In 1975, I was sent to Kesh where I was in remand in a cage
with some of the other loyalist detainees.
There were thousands of prisoners.
We had classes in guitar, English, maths, gym,
bomb-making, weapons training and marching.
The UDA and UVF had separate compounds.
It was an uneasy truce, but one of the strangest things about
Long Kesh was how we cooperated with our enemy
if we needed something.

To get messages to our guys in the other cages,
we'd unscrew the metal bed ends and stuff messages into them.
Then we'd throw the ends to the IRA cage next to us and they'd
throw it to the UVF who'd throw to the Official IRA,
and then to the UDA.
It was cooperation between enemies, all done in trust.
We didn't look at their messages,
and to my knowledge, they never looked at ours.

The day I left prison I cried like a baby.
It was the brotherhood.

*I didn't know one man
out of the eighty-four loyalists
in our compound who didn't cry when they left.*

*Even the most notorious murderers wept.
Even the hardest of the hard.*

*I was terrified, utterly petrified of leaving.
It was 1976, and the Troubles were roaring bad.
There had been a lot of drive-by shootings
and I was always on guard,
afraid that the IRA would shoot me.
Afraid that the UDA would take me out.*

*One night I came home after being at my girlfriend's,
turned the front door key, and took a half pace.
And as the door opened, I heard:
#!/%!!@##!!!*

*The milk bottles exploded.
They'd been waiting for me.
If I hadn't taken that extra step,
they would have shot me through the heart.
They missed by just a few inches.*

*A month or two later, I came home late at night and
I heard a car pull into the street.
My heart was thumping out of my chest.
I heard the door close. I ran and got my father's shotgun,
put a cartridge in and waited on the third stair in the hallway.
Footsteps were coming.
I could see a head bobbing up and down through the glass door.
I was just about to shoot, when I heard a cough
and realised it was my sister coming home.
If she hadn't coughed, I would have blasted her to bits.
I was wrecked.*

When I look back now, I realise
that I've had roughly thirty-three friends murdered.
It was a terrible time.
Such a waste of life.

Somehow though, I was able to walk away from it all.
I have no explanation for how things changed,
other than after my release, it was April.
I remember the beauty of the leaves on the trees
and the smell of freshness in the air.
I'd been surrounded by concrete for years.
It was like switching one light off and another one on.
Lighting my way to a better future.

I got married and had my own children,
and was determined that they wouldn't follow in my footsteps.
For a long time, I protected them,
not wanting them to have any knowledge of what I'd done.
I sugar-coated things out of kindness and love,
but maybe I also was afraid
that it would change what they thought of me.
I was afraid they'd lose their respect.
It was my veil of shame.

But I wanted them to hear it from me
rather than taking the chance that
someone else would tell them.
So, when they were both seventeen,
I took them to where it all had happened.
I sat them down and told them what I'd done.
It was probably one of the hardest things I've ever done in my life.
Picking over the bones of war.

Ripples

> *It was probably one of the hardest things*
> *I've ever done in my life.*
>
> *Picking over the bones of war.*

The early tragedy in James' life began at the River Faughn, and rippled outward in concentric circles, touching all aspects of his existence.

When James first shared this story with me in an early meeting in 2009, we were both in tears. It was the first time he had ever spoken of it, and once he started, the floodgates opened. I was overwhelmed that this eleven-year-old boy had held this tragedy inside himself all these years. He had learned to be silent at great cost to his emotional well being. No one had cared for or comforted him, or even asked how he was doing. He had learned to manage his memories and guilt by keeping it all in.

James believes that the unprocessed trauma may be what led him to join a loyalist paramilitary group as a teenager. While he hadn't been able to save Thomas from drowning, perhaps by joining the UDA, he could save his people.

Embodiment

During the production, James sat on the side of the stage as he related his story, while Fionnbharr played the part of the younger James. For me, this was one of the surprising gifts of the project. It came about almost by accident. Fionnbharr, whose father had been assassinated by suspected loyalist and police collusion, distrusted James from the beginning. So much so, that he was fearful of sleeping in the same room with him during our cast residential.

But both were smokers, and spent many hours outside together on break, rolling cigarettes, and having good craic. Fionnbharr respected James' honesty, and slowly over the weeks and months, the two became mates. By the time he played the younger James onstage, he was able to fully embody him, including his emotions of terror and grief. It was a beautiful example of walking in the 'other's' shoes.

Shame and Courage

James was one of the first people in our group to display vulnerability.

> *The first time I told the story to the group, I was shaking like a leaf and I was almost physically sick.*

Sharing his story in a group that included republicans and police took courage. A quality that James has displayed since he was a young child, when, with no thought about the danger to himself, he waded in the swirling river waters to try and save Thomas. Many years later, in our group, he bravely confronted his long-buried wounds of grief and shame. Shame for not being able to save Thomas from drowning, shame for his involvement in the UDA, and shame and grief for the injury his friend sustained when the bomb they were building went off. Being accountable and vulnerable both within our group, and then in public, took enormous courage.

> *My past was a big bag of shame*
> *I've carried around like Gulliver towing his warships in the Lilliputian sea.*
> *I've finally let it go.*

James, in company with all the Theatre of Witness performers, understood the chances they were taking in going public. Even though the country was ostensibly at peace, the Troubles were still reverberating. Paramilitaries remained active, and ex-combatants who spoke out were in real and present danger. Those who were currently or previously members of the security forces were under explicit death threats.

None of us knew what would happen at any show. There was the very real fear that violence would break out. When we were in the early stages of creating the production, the participants began to recognise what they all were going to reveal. James voiced what everyone had been thinking:

> I don't know if you, Teya, realise how dangerous this is.
> Probably they do on the other side of the table.
> But this is dangerous beyond dangerous.
> Maybe we are the ones who are brave enough to
> stick our heads above the parapet.

Accountability

Theatre of Witness is a long process of trust building. Trust within oneself, with others, and then trust in the process. After we had completed the tour of the original production, we were offered more opportunities to perform at peace conferences and other venues. Somehow, at that point, James had the courage to publicly take more accountability for his actions during the Troubles. He altered his introduction to describe himself as a convicted terrorist.

Naming himself a terrorist in Northern Ireland took courage that is rare to witness. There are many ex-combatants, loyalist and republican, who would be greatly offended by the implication that they were terrorists rather than freedom fighters. But James, steadfast in his own sense of truth, chose the stance of accountability.

> I stand before you as a father, a grandfather
> and a peacemaker.

But I actually stand before you as a convicted terrorist.
And I don't say that lightly,
and I don't say that with any pride.
People have challenged me, saying,
"We weren't terrorists, we were combatants".

But when I've spoken to people,
the very people we thought we were protecting.
They see it differently.
We restricted their movements.
We told them what they could and couldn't do,
who they could and couldn't see,
and on many occasions, held them prisoners
in their own homes.
They lived in terror.
And that makes us terrorists.

Widening Ripples of Peace

A few years after the production and film of *We Carried Your Secrets* toured, James was invited to the dedication of the pedestrian Peace Bridge linking the Cityside and Waterside of Derry. Beforehand, he spoke on a panel showcasing the effects of the EU's peace monies in Northern Ireland. Johannes Hann, the European Commissioner for Regional Policy was there to dedicate the bridge.

I just spoke from my heart.

Pauline Ross (Director of The Playhouse) asked me to meet her at the City Hotel in ten minutes. I asked her what it was about and she said, "I'll tell you what it's about when you get there". When I arrived, she said that I would be speaking to the head of the EU. "What will I say?" I asked.

"I trust you. You're always good." And not ten minutes later,

I was at the conference, representing The Playhouse Theatre of Witness programme which had been funded by the EU.

I was utterly terrified and was shaking. The only brief I was given was to talk about the Theatre of Witness, the Peace Bridge and to thank the EU for supporting those projects. I got up and stood at the lectern and all of a sudden, with no preparation, I just spoke from my heart.

I told my story about growing up on one side of the river and how I was influenced to join a paramilitary. I talked about the fear I had had to come to the Cityside and how Theatre of Witness had broken down so many barriers within our group – loyalist, republican and security forces. I spoke about how the Peace Bridge was now a now a vital corridor linking two communities who had lived on opposite sides of a liquid barrier. How the monies contributed by the EU really were creating peace.

The whole place erupted in applause. Johannes Hann came up to me and said: "That is the most passionate speech I've heard in thirty years. I'd like to bring you to the EU to further our work." Then we went to the bridge and cut the ribbon.

I now stand before you, a man who takes responsibility for the damage I caused.

A year later Commissioner Hann invited us to Brussels to perform for the EU. We showed Victoria and Fionnbharr's parts from *We Carried Your Secrets* on film, and Kathleen and James performed live. James began with his introduction about being a terrorist and told the story of joining the UDA, being in prison, and finally released.

After getting out of prison,
there was some pressure for me to become reinvolved.
But I knew it was wrong.
I knew I couldn't go back to it.
I knew it wasn't the way forward.
But there was nobody showing me what to do.

Peace was basically a dirty word.

Then I had a chance meeting with a man
who I suppose shone a light on a different path.
He was working with young people,
teaching them to respect each other
and to respect the views of others,
and in a very quiet way with no fuss.
I worked with him for five years.
But during all that time,
I buried my past.
It was a secret I kept close.

I was paralysed with shame, until I met Teya
and began working on 'We Carried Your Secrets'.

She teased my story out of me and I told her things
I'd never told anyone,
including my own family. Even my wife at the time.
Eventually I shared my story in our small group,
and then onstage in front of thousands of people.
It was one of the most positive things I'd ever experienced.
My shame was laid bare, and I wasn't judged.

I now stand before you,
a man who takes responsibility for the damage I caused.
A man who has walked deeply into his past,
picking over the bones of a war.
A man who has been set free.

James later told me there were also ripple effects for his family after he shared his story. He had long-needed conversations with his sisters. And his former wife lauded him on a local radio show, acknowledging the healing she saw in him. He and his children had more open conversations. James himself grew in confidence and continued to build on his desire to facilitate workshops, especially for youth the same age as he had been when he got caught up. He performed in Utrecht and London, as well as over the border in the Republic.

Touching Greatness

Then came the opportunity of a lifetime. US Congressman and civil rights icon, John Lewis, and the current police chief of Montgomery Alabama, Kevin Murphy, came to Derry to talk about race relations. We were invited to present Theatre of Witness at the gathering where the congressman and police chief spoke.

Congressman Lewis recounted the horror of the 1961 violent white supremacist mob attack in Montgomery, when he was among the Freedom Riders who had come to protest segregation. Then he and Chief Murphy spoke about the public apology Murphy made in 2013 for his department's failure to protect the Freedom Riders. In a heartfelt gesture, Murphy had taken the police badge off his own uniform and presented it to Lewis. They both spoke tearfully about it that day in Derry. Their profoundly moving story offered real inspiration for the possibilities of peacebuilding.

Following their talk, James spoke about his own journey towards peace, from being a convicted terrorist to committing his life to peace. Afterwards, Congressman Lewis expressed how moved he had been by his testimony and invited James to visit him at the US Congress. When James told him that, as a convicted terrorist, he wasn't legally allowed into the United States, Congressman Lewis offered to help.

True to his word, John Lewis paved the way for James to come to Washington DC in 2015. James drove the same route the Freedom Riders had taken down South, and ended his journey with a meeting with the congressman. They spent a few hours together, and as James affirms, they became friends.

> *Coming away from Congressman John Lewis was like knowing deep down inside you had just witnessed greatness. He radiated something – serenity. We gave each other a hug with great feeling. It was a life changer for me. It's one of those things that fits into your life – a great positive change. I learned so much from how he spoke. His language was not challenging. Our time together was just between two men.*
>
> *We talked about young people. He told me that in preparation for the lunch counter sit-ins that Freedom Summer, they had done a lot of training. "We sat on stools and beat the heck out of those sitting, so they wouldn't break under pressure." I don't what it takes to get kids to be that passionate about something now. I fear that those days are lost.*
>
> *Even though he was such a huge political and historical figure, he was humble. His parents were sharecroppers. He was reared with nothing. His father had died when he was a kid. But he rose to a level that no one could imagine. It was the way he spoke; what he was saying, I felt it comforted me. It was like eating ice cream. We related to each other on the social justice level without it being talked about in those terms. But there was a connection there.*
>
> *On the back of my experiences with Theatre of Witness, which made me more accepting of others and more willing to accept other's points of view, meeting John was the icing on the cake.*
>
> **Coming away from Congressman John Lewis was like knowing deep down inside, you had just witnessed greatness.**

A Ripple Effect From the Other Side

Even after more than forty years,
Thomas is never far away from my thoughts.

Thirteen years of performances, presentations and workshops had helped to heal much of the trauma of James' early life experiences. But just like there is a never-ending flow of ripples in a river, the healing of trauma unfolds in layers and waves. One never knows when a memory, thought or emotion will rise and emerge again.

Following the premiere performance of *We Carried Your Secrets* in 2009, Eamonn Baker, a community peacebuilder from the other side (nationalist/Catholic), approached James and told him how deeply touched he had been. "For me, as someone from a different tradition, I don't want you to carry these bags of shame. I want you to let them go. You felt enough pain."

Eamonn explained how being a witness to James' story onstage had deeply moved him. They began a friendship that has continued to deepen over time.

Thirteen years later James took Eamonn back to the river where he had watched Thomas drown.

> *Even after more than forty years, Thomas is never far away from my thoughts. One day I asked Eamonn if we could walk to the River Faughn. It was intimate. I said, "I'm taking you here showing you, and you are the only person". I had never had taken anyone to the river where my story happened. It was sacred. I felt protected.*
>
> *I was able to point my finger and say, "Thomas fell in there. Sam fell in here. I ran up here." I was staring at the water. The passageway between Thomas falling in and being lost was only seventy-five yards. Most of it was shallow, except where the current pulled him into the deep waters.*
>
> *I could see Eamonn reduced to tears and I could see he was*

feeling the impact of what I was saying. The impact was almost physical in his facial and bodily emotions. He was absorbing the pain.

I told them the story from an awfully vulnerable place from within myself. I was sharing it, not as James the sixty-five-year-old man, but as an eleven- year-old boy. Eamon didn't interrupt.

As I gave him the gift of the story, he just stood there and listened. It was another ripple effect of being witnessed. Being witnessed from the physical place where it happened. It turned into something positive for healing. It was almost sacred. I felt the weight lifting.

I felt liberated.

Epiphany

That liberation has come in waves. Long after all the events in this chapter happened, I was in a virtual small break-out room with James as we presented a Theatre of Witness workshop to business leaders from Denmark. I thought I knew the 'bones' of James' story. And although I felt confident he would keep it fresh and speak from his heart, I wasn't expecting to be surprised by the content of what he shared.

It happened when a participant asked him if he could pinpoint the exact moment when his transformation began. James got a faraway look in his eyes, then recounted a new memory which had me in tears. It was the story about the epiphany he experienced in the Crumlin Road prison when he was just nineteen. This recollection was absolutely central to James' transformation, but one that he had kept close since 1974.

To give you a picture – the cell I was in was supposed to house one person. But we were in three-deep on every side. Our beds were just eighteen inches away from each other. It was crammed full. Our sanitation was a bucket in the corner and a two-gallon jug of water. I was terrified.

Billy had red hair, rosy cheeks and was wearing a brown leather jacket. I don't use his real name, because I don't want the story to be filtered back to his family even now all these years later. We met the first day I was in my cell. He looked at me with an appeal in his eyes, almost gesturing for me to come to him.

You never asked anyone why they were in prison, but he started telling me that he had committed murder. He had been sent by the UDA to kill a shopkeeper in another part of the country. It was a small corner shop. The guy came in from his dwelling and Billy shot him. Then the shopkeeper's wife came in, saw her husband lying on the floor, mortally wounded, and she started screaming. Billy shot her too. Then, in walked their eight-year-old daughter. She saw her mother and father on the floor bleeding and in the throes of dying and she started screaming and running around the shop. Billy ran after her firing his gun.

When he got to this part of the story, I turned sheet white. I was afraid to know, but I asked him what happened, and he said he'd run out of ammunition. The look on his face was like he had failed his mission. I was horrified. We had ethics. We didn't kill women and children. Who would want to kill an eight-year-old child? Right after that, I walked away and lay on my bunk for a couple of hours.

Life changed then and there. How could the 'effing' organisation that I was part of justify killing a child? I thought, I can't be part of this. I would have ended up being just like him.

I had been a tough guy, but I knew then and there that I'd devote my life to finding a peaceful path forward when I got out. It was the greatest decision I ever made.

> *I never told anyone about Billy for a long, long time. When I do share the story now, people ask me, "Why do you think he picked you to tell the story to?" I don't know the answer. I don't like to use the word epiphany because it's religious and I'm not. But it was almost a holy happening.*

When James shared this in our recent workshop, I was once again reminded of the mysterious qualities of ripple effects. So often we don't know the impact a shared story may have on someone. Billy took his own life and never knew that he had forever transformed James' path. And James may never know the effects his stories will have on us.

Peacebuilding is like dancing the waltz.
Sometimes you push and sometimes you yield...

And sometimes you don't feel
like you're moving at all.

Robin, *We Carried Your Secrets*

A Letter to My Unborn Grandchild

Jon

2008. It is my daughter's wedding rehearsal.
I take her arm to practice walking her down the church aisle.
After a few steps, I can't move anymore.
Tears flood me.
It is the first time in forty years that I've walked the length of that church without carrying a coffin.
At what should be one of the happiest days of my life,
all I can see is forty years of coffins that I've carried
down that same aisle.
My daughter puts her arms around me. "It's OK Daddy."
Is it OK?

I walk around this town every day.
I walk the walls and the streets, and I still see the battles
that we fought, the bullet holes in walls.
I hear the screams.
I smell the CS gas.
Some days it seems like it was all just yesterday.

I look into the eyes of the guys of my generation.
And I think, if it hadn't been for this conflict,
what was your potential?

I remember so many of them as great footballers,
artists, mechanics…
But it's all locked down there without an avenue.
What was useful in these guys has been used up.
The war used it up.
Prison used it up.
And drink used it up.
I see it in their eyes.
Flashes of stories that can't be told.
Ghosts.

My tenth grandchild is due to be born
and I think about the stories of these men.
I think about mine.

To you, my unborn grandchild, I've written you a letter.
The first of many that I hope we will share.
I want to pass on some of this history.
I want you to know who your grandfather was
before he became Granda.

As a young boy, I used to dream that I would become
an Air Force pilot like my father.
Flying off to Africa, America, Australia,
meeting people from all over the world.
But those were the dreams of a 'home boy',
who grew up in an orphanage.
In reality, my father had been injured
and was sent away to hospital.
He ended up on the streets.
My mother had a nervous breakdown and
someone made a decision to put us in a Home.
From age two-and-a-half to thirteen, I wasn't a name.
I was number ten,
standing in line with the other boys, in that hellhole called a Home.

It was a place of great paradox.
An institution meant for care, with a lot of religion,
but little faith.
And immense anger and cruelty within its walls.

So I dreamed.
Some days I'd sit up on the banks of the Foyle and
watch the salmon leap.
There I'd dream of my father in shining armour coming to rescue
me with the keys to freedom.
I'd watch those salmon jump like they were magic,
knowing I'd never want to catch anything as beautiful as that.
Freedom.

In the mid-sixties, after nearly eleven years, my mother got out of
hospital and we were reunited as family.
A family of strangers.
I'd been cloistered for so many years and was
hungry to learn the ways of the world.
In America, the Civil Rights Movement was in full swing,
and I was inspired by the stories of
Martin Luther King and Rosa Parks
struggling for freedom for their people.

When they talked about Civil Rights in Derry,
at first I didn't yet see any connection between their struggle
and ours.
But in the Bogside, disenfranchised working class Catholics
were living in appalling overcrowded conditions and
suffering from third world diseases.
Polio, rickets and tuberculosis were rampant.

Then, I went to the first Civil Rights march.
I learned about The Corporation
and the city's system of gerrymandering.

How Catholics were being denied jobs, housing and votes.
In Derry, thirty thousand women were working in shirt factories,
But over 60% of Catholic men were unemployed.
All of a sudden, things began to make sense.

I'd spent ten years in a Boys' Home,
not because my mother didn't love me,
but because, although she left school at age fourteen
and went to the factory,
she couldn't have a house because of The Corporation.
To give a Catholic a house meant to give them a vote.
They weren't in the business of giving votes to Catholics,
and they didn't build housing.

At that point, any other dreams I had for myself
went out the window.
I wanted to take it all on.
The Corporation, the police, the government.
It was about fairness and justice.
The option of letting someone else fight for me wasn't an option.

August 1969. The Battle of the Bogside

Young people got empowered and the police overreacted.
The fight became a rite of passage for young men.
The complete and utter mayhem that erupted became
a call to arms for so many of us.
I decided to join the IRA because,
when the time came, and it would,
I wasn't going to stand against the forces of the State
with only stones or petrol bombs.
I would meet them on their own terms.
I became a warrior standing on the street corner
defending my community
with a rifle in my hand and balaclava covering my face.
I didn't go to war,
they brought the war to me.

Then came internment, house raids, torture, more protests.
Friends and neighbours started dying.
It seemed to merge into one big mess in my head.
We went from protests to pistols, from bottles to bombs.

Bloody Sunday

A massacre.
Thirteen people killed in just eighteen minutes.
One in front, one behind and one alongside of me.
Screams and pure terror.
People just being slaughtered.
In Ecclesiastes it says: "There's time for everything.
A time to be born,
A time to die.
A time for war,
A time for peace.
A time to kill,
A time to heal."
Tell me if there's a time to watch a fifteen-year-old shot,
not just once, but shot again when he's on the ground?
Tell me if there's a time for grandparents, mothers and fathers
to bury their children?
Tell me if there's time to listen to an entire city cry for their dead?

The funerals. Thirteen coffins. It lasted three days.
Fifty, sixty, seventy thousand people crying.
Even the heavens cried.
And the aftermath - empty shoes, fresh flowers
and the rain
washing blood down the drains.

It left me wanting to kill.
You begin to dehumanise.
It's not a person. It's the uniform, the number, the name.

He's just a soldier, just a peeler, just an off-duty cop.

They all became faceless.
They all became the enemy.

I remember people saying
"It will stop when the first child dies.
It will stop when the first policeman dies,
The first soldier,
The first priest,
The first woman."
But it didn't stop,
And it all fuelled the anger and started more waves of retaliation.
I watched young men grow old too quickly.
And some not get to grow old at all.
We were in a cycle that seemed impossible to stop.

Things began to pile up on me.
Physically I was a wreck and emotionally I was burned out.
I decided that I was past the point of
being of use to any organisation.
I was more of a liability.
So, I stepped out for a while.
I went south where I drank and partied too much.
But it allowed me to be a teenager for a while and
come back with more perspective.

My focus changed.
I realised that conflict wasn't ever going to be solved
by building bigger and bigger bombs.
We now had a city completely polarised.
They say up to twenty thousand members of the Protestant
community had left the west bank.
And we were now further away from achieving the
civil rights agenda than when we started.
We, who were responsible for tearing the city apart,
now had find ways to put it together again.
Jon the fighter, became the Jon the community worker.

New Year's Eve 1978. I met the girl who was to become my wife.
Your grandmother.
We dated only three weeks before I asked,
"What are you doing over the weekend?"
She said she wasn't sure.
"Well, do you fancy getting married then?"
Amazingly she said "yes."
And over thirty years and nine children later,
we await the arrival of you.

But our family has paid the price for my passion.
Your older aunts and uncles were often abused
because of what I was involved in.
I didn't consult your granny, and left her alone raising nine kids
while I was off trying to save the world instead of saving the family.
I went off to Ukraine when your aunt Lisa was eleven.
She often feels that I put the whole world ahead of her.
"Is my daddy out there to fight someone else's war?
Is he coming home?"

During the Bloody Sunday Inquiry, I began to really lose it.
I was flooded with images, and I started drinking and not sleeping.
I couldn't look at the kids. Could barely hold a conversation.
They've had to live with an absent and broken father.

I walk this city and I see its potential.
I see the possibilities for peace and justice.
But when I walk in the Bogside,
I also see the litter and broken bottles.
I see lost youth sitting on the walls,
Looking for freedom and identity in graffiti, flags and drink.
They want someone to see them, to know they're there.
They want to be men.

Fighters.
Heroes.

*At age seventeen or eighteen, standing with the disenfranchised
was our rite of passage.
It's what gave us voice and turned us into men.
What rites of passage are left for these young men?
Do they know they're walking on sacred ground?
To you, my unborn grandchild,
I hope that the world we leave you will be a better place.*

Granda

Generation to Generation

I used to live in another world

Jon's then unborn granddaughter is now a teenager. His numerous children, grandchildren and great-grandchildren have now heard many of his stories – some for the first time through seeing Theatre of Witness productions or films. They know the world he inhabited and the legacy he has left. They understand the dreams he has for them, as well as for children all over the world. They have a grandfather who has devoted his life to civil rights and peace, albeit first through violence and now through dialogue, teaching and Theatre of Witness.

> *I dedicated my part in the show to my granddaughter who hadn't been born yet. I wanted to let her know that behind just being her Granda, there was something else.*

> *It is like peeling an onion where one story leads to another. A whole life woven in history.*

> **Theatre of Witness has put flesh on the bones of society's memory that the next generations are supposed to carry on.**

Northern Ireland has more than two thousand unsolved cases related to the Troubles. As the decades have passed, many people fighting these cases have been the children and grandchildren of victims. But recently the State decided to draw a line under any cases that happened before 1998 when the Peace Agreement was signed. That means there are myriad families who still don't have the answers they have so desperately been seeking for thirty or forty years. They want to know what happened to their loved ones. And who was responsible.

All of those answers are lost now, except for the opportunities that people themselves take to share their stories.

It takes bravery on behalf of victims and families to say to ex-combatants, "I really do want to hear what you have to say. I really do want to know."

Politics isn't working, because it's not getting that connection that needs to be made in society. What we need to do is bring it down and bring it down and bring it down. And for me, politics was always going to be local. It was always going to be about community.

We need to get those stories within communities to start transforming.

Trauma

Jon, like so many people in Northern Ireland and around the world, has been a victim and survivor, as well as an ex-combatant. He grew up in extreme poverty, suffered institutional abuse, and joined the IRA to fight for the civil rights of his people. In the middle of a war, one of his early strategies for trying to get justice was through guns and bombs.

Like many ex-combatants, once the peace treaty was signed, he began fighting for justice in new ways. For him, it was through politics, national and international teaching, and Theatre of Witness. I believe it's because he's been on both sides of the survivor/perpetrator continuum that he is perfectly placed to dedicate his life to reconciliation and education.

In an early iteration of our original script, Jon shared more of his childhood trauma related to institutional abuse. When he was living in the Home, one of the nuns beat him on the head with a broomstick so hard that the stick went through his skull. The injury left him with permanent brain damage. To this day, he struggles with learning difficulties and memory issues. Some of his siblings suffered even worse fates. His indefatigable fight for justice and acknowledgment has been on behalf of all the victims and survivors in Northern Ireland.

For Jon, being in *We Carried Your Secrets* was an avenue for him to share the many causes and conditions that led to his being active in the conflict. It also allowed him to become a model for peace-making, by showing the deep relationships he developed with the cast members from all sides.

Enduring great deprivation, childhood abuse, and living through a raging war, have forged the empathy and compassion Jon feels towards all who have endured similar circumstances, no matter which side they were on. It's made him want to fight on their behalf. But now, rather than do battle as a warrior with violence, he works tirelessly for political causes. Jon is also known for being a compelling teacher of the history of Northern Ireland.

> *We, who were responsible for tearing the city apart, now had find ways to put it together again.*
>
> *Jon the fighter, has become Jon the community worker.*
>
> *Our job as peacemakers is not to fix things, but to allow other people the space where they can be uplifted.*
>
> **We all need to be lifted up.**

Heroism

When Jon gives talks, he sometimes speaks of two different kinds of heroism. The first is a quiet version, built on compassion and humanitarian principles of care:

> *On Bloody Sunday, there were people lifting people who were dying who they didn't know. Around the world, we see these images of people carrying somebody. That's a human strength that you should never have to prove. You should never have to prove that you can do it, or that you have a heart.*
>
> *You do it because, in fact, sometimes you do stuff like that. It's the human spirit triumphing over adversity and triumphing over horror. And in its midst, we are going to find the quiet heroes. And a lot of them just melt back to the background and are never heard from again.*

Jon's favourite image from *We Carried Your Secrets* is from the Bloody Sunday scene when Fionnbharr lies in Kieran's arms. Jon calls it 'the Pieta moment'; the non-verbal expression of surrender and quiet heroism made visible.

When he spoke about it, memories of a similar image flooded him. It was the statue in the Home where he lived for many years, showing Mary cradling her dead son Jesus after he has been taken down from the Cross.

> *There was a copy of Michelangelo's Pieta at the children's home where I was raised. I didn't notice it until I was forty years of age. In Michelangelo's actual Pieta, Mary is in scale to the form of the adult Jesus.*
>
> *We all have that image of a mother holding her child. In our minds, the mother is always going to be larger than her child. But my own mother was a tiny woman and I am over 6'6".*
>
> *However if the statue at the Home had been done to scale, Mary could never have been able to hold Jesus the way she held him. So that particular sculpture in the Home is the Madonna and child, not Jesus and his mother. I think that*

> *statue gives honour to the mother's view.*

For Jon, the Pieta moment in *We Carried Your Secrets* reverberates with religious symbolism, brokenness, surrender and being lifted up. The hero is the one doing the lifting. The one who displays love, comfort, and grief. The mother. The Madonna.

The second kind of heroism is the sort often written about in history books. A warrior valour that lauds people for going into battle for a cause.

> *There's no denying that there was a lot of heroism in the conflict. But that's not what I want my children, grandchildren and their friends to be focussing on. I want them to understand the experience, to try and learn from it. To understand the cost of it.*
>
> **We've got cemeteries full of heroes. And we've got prisons full of heroes.**
>
> *I want them to see that even though I was out there fighting, there was another way, as I was eventually to claim.*
>
> **The force of argument is really greater than the argument of force.**
>
> *Each of us, and each community would want to believe that they had a monopoly of the pain and the suffering of this conflict. But, through listening to the other story, you realise you don't have a monopoly. This war impacted everybody.*

Jon has a wide perspective about the arc of history. He contextualises the conflict in Northern Ireland in relationship to human rights struggles around the world. He studies peace processes, civil rights and leadership. He no longer wants to glorify war in any way.

> *What will be future of the political aspect be, other than continuing with the myth, the legend and the themes of the past? It's part of the story, but don't make it that story.*
>
> **Overcoming. That's the story.**

Joining Theatre of Witness

Jon became part of the cast of *We Carried Your Secrets* after we had already established relationships and been working together for a while. When he joined, his openness, vulnerability and credentials as an ex-IRA combatant who was now working for peace stood him in good stead. He already had a connection with Robin, but quickly became friends with everyone else.

I knew his actual story would be powerful, but I don't think I grasped how fully he'd take to the artistic process of creating the show. He was quick to give supportive feedback to each performer whenever he saw something that moved him.

At Victoria's suggestion, he took the whole group on a walking tour of the city to recognise and honour the sacred places where people had died. He took accountability for what he had done during the Troubles and was willing to let his grief speak truthfully. He took up the mantle of being a living teacher of history about the city of Derry.

> *As an ex-combatant, you get to a point where you're not afraid of the past. You overcome that fear that made you almost put your head down because you were embarrassed by what you did. It shouldn't have happened. We never should have had to make those choices. But we made the choices, and we live with the consequences.*

The Centre of the Wound

> *It's important to visit the wound and know why you want to move forward.*

Telling one's traumatic story through Theatre of Witness brings performers right back to the moment they are depicting onstage. The centre of the wound. But instead of being at the mercy of the event, they have a creative scaffolding surrounding them. The script and stage directions act like a road map. Performers know what they are going to say, where and how they will move and what comes next. The words, music and physical directions give them something concrete and stable to hold on to. Sometimes we had to find creative solutions for how to do that.

After rehearsing for a while with Jon, I realised that his head injury and extreme trauma were making it difficult for him to retain memorised lines. We decided together to shape his part into the form of a written letter to his unborn grandchild that he could read onstage. This freed him from the pressure of having to think and allowed him to go deep into the emotions of his story. His reading of the letter became scaffolding he could hold on to.

When I'm creating a scene, I also make sure to build in moments of support so that performers can pull themselves outside of the intensity of their trauma. Sometimes it is in the form of scripted words that propel them into a place of witnessing rather than re-experiencing. Other times, physical connections to fellow performers help them come back to the present moment. In addition, cast members will have rehearsed their parts so many times, that they can trust the trajectory of the scene to take them from the deep wound into a place of strength and resilience.

In Jon's case, as he narrated his story from the side, performers onstage animated many of the scenes physically. This gave him the opportunity to feel and witness his own story coming to life, while at the same time, absorbing the commitment and support of the group.

> *Even now, telling my story - it brings you back to the wound. But you're not stuck at the wound and there's a support network. It's important to visit the wound and know why you want to move forward.*

Now, thirteen years after the show, when Jon watches his part on film or retells his story in workshops, he still gets choked up.

> *I would have hoped at this point, which is now thirty to thirty-five years of talking a lot about the Troubles and my own history, that I would be able to put this out here without getting emotional. I can't. I still find myself choking up and I still find myself wiping a tear away.*

Commodification of Stories

Because Theatre of Witness in Northern Ireland has been successful, it continues to grow. Numerous national and international opportunities to offer workshops are being offered to the performers. As time goes by, the stories can become commodified by those organising the workshops and presentations.

Producers might assume that the performers always want to share their stories. They may not think through what the impact may be on the storytellers. But the cost of sharing one's story is always there. Performers open personal and societal wounds that need to be constantly honoured, respected and cared for. All these years later, they need tending to just as much as they did when we first began. These stories are sacred gifts.

> *What has the conflict done to us? It isn't cost-free to talk about it. It's just like opening an envelope, reading the letter, putting it back in the envelope, and then putting the envelope back in a filing cabinet. That's not the way that happens. Every time something like this happens, you take a piece of somebody's soul with it.*

The manner in which the performers' stories get used and framed, long after the original productions have concluded, is also critical. How do we keep the essence of the stories pure? How do we ensure that the intention of this work to serve peace is always front and centre? Both in the content of the workshops, as well as in the way that the performers are treated and cared for?

Jon is always thinking about the impact of Theatre of Witness on audiences, and the importance of not glorifying violence, history or the performers themselves.

> *Sometimes somebody asks me to do a workshop, not realising what it takes. "Ach Jon, all you have to do is go and turn the video on." I couldn't do that. I have to set people up so they can understand. So that when they leave here, they're thinking about transformation.*
>
> *I want to make sure that they're thinking, not about the journey that I've been on, but the one they are now on. Because if the story goes from me, it's no longer mine. It's theirs.*
>
> *The audience shouldn't be asking, "How much did I enjoy that?" Their first question should be, "How much did I learn from that?"*

Showing Peace

How do we model making an informed choice?

The question of how to impart the complexities of the Troubles is difficult. As Jon describes, it's easy to show violence. But he has wondered: how do you show peace?

> *We are modelling peace when we do the Theatre of Witness Peace workshops at schools. Sometimes the students are looking for excitement, blood and guts and ask, "When did the first bomb go off?"* **But a lot of the conflict was making nothing happen. How do you show that?**

> *We can show the adrenaline rush when we were on the way to do something violent. But how do we model making an informed choice? I know what those violent choices lead to, but young people today don't have that.*

In the end, Jon's commitment to the Theatre of Witness process has increased through time. He never slows and can often be found travelling up and down Ireland, as well as abroad, to share his story with students of diverse backgrounds and nationalities. He traded in his former identity and has grown into being a man devoted to peacebuilding, justice and teaching.

> *The whole Theatre of Witness journey has been about growth. It's about personal growth, spiritual growth, and the growth of the knowledge and understanding. And knowing the place to use it.*

I Once Knew a Girl

The Stories of Women Affected
by the Troubles
Created and Performed in 2010

Therese
Anne
Kathleen

Sanctuary

Refugees and Those
Living Without Homes in NI
Created and Performed in 2013

Therese

Sanctuary

Therese McCann

I Once Knew a Girl

When I was a little girl, I wanted to be a gymnast, a dancer,
or a PE teacher.
I never learned to read in school and thought I was stupid.
But when I danced, I felt alive and free.

The Troubles started when I was seven.
We lived off the Shankill Road.
Back then we used to play with the Protestants.
We'd go to their bonfires and parties,
and we'd play wee games together in the streets.
Then the shooting began.
It was terrifying because you had to get from one wee place
to another.
My daddy used to say, "If they start shooting, go to the ground!"
So you were always hiding behind him,
trying to get from one street to another.
The ground was burnt black where all the cars had been set on fire.

One July morning, I remember Daddy telling us that
trouble was starting
and we should stay away from the bonfires.
He went off to work and Mammy was in the kitchen
boiling nappies.
"Don't go!"

Then we heard shootings.
That night there were gangs outside the house.
"We know you're in there hiding in the dark, you Fenians!
We're not stupid!"
Mammy told us, "I'm going to get Granda.
If I'm not back in 10 minutes, you'll know I've been shot."
We were all terrified, crying and squealing.

Another time Daddy came in and said he'd been told that
we were being put out.
The front door was open
and I saw a big gun facing the house.
Mammy ran into the street shouting,
"You were supposed to be our friends. Now you're putting us out?"
The car was too small for our things.
The only thing Mammy lifted was the sewing machine.
Mammy had no coat.
We went to Daddy's sisters. My aunt gave her a coat,
but they said there was no room for us.
We ended up in the Holy Child School,
where it seemed like there were thousands of other families.
I stuck to my Mammy like glue.
I was quiet, but I was always listening.
I still always listen.

My aunt tried to go back into our house the next day,
but it was cordoned off.
The soldiers told her that there was nothing left to it.
"We saw them taking the furniture, light it on fire
and dance around it while it burned.
There's another family living in the house now."

We were like refugees.
No one wanted to take us in.
Finally, we got shipped to Dublin to a Ra family for nine months,
but they eventually put us out too,

'cos they thought we were bringing the Troubles with us.
Mammy used to cry all the time.
She was always so sad.

We kept moving and getting put out.
When we lived in Antrim, we went to a Protestant school where
they'd shout, "Fenians, you're in our school!
Stop taking our classrooms!"
If us Catholics were standing alone at the bus stop,
the driver would just drive right past us.
So we'd skip school and go play in the woods.
I never learned to read properly until I was thirty-seven.

Finally, the Ra got us a two-bedroom house back in the Falls,
and we stopped going to school altogether.
The house was a nightmare. It was run down and stank.
The toilet never worked and the paper was hanging off the walls.
We had to move rugs over the holes in the floor.
I was always ashamed, and I hated it.
My father was in the Knights of Malta,
and we weren't allowed to go into the front room,
'cos that's where the men came when they were wounded.
There were weapons there too.
It was a republican safe house.
But it wasn't safe for us.

At night I had awful nightmares about men coming to get me.
I would cuddle up with my Mummy and stay awake all night.
She was always so sad.
I'd brush her hair for hours and watch her sleep.
When I was eleven,
I'd make breakfast for my five brothers and sisters
and get them out to school.
Then I'd come home and do the cleaning and light the fire.

I just wanted to make Mammy happy.

*I tried to make everything spotless and lovely
So she'd praise me and see that I existed.
But she never did.*

*Mammy liked to gamble and was always going out to bingo.
When I was making breakfast, my uncle just lay there
smelling of cigarettes.
He lay there with dirty black socks.
He'd whisper in my ear and touch me.
But no one else ever saw.
And no one believed.*

*The worst thing that happened to me then
was at my Granny's house.
My cousin took me there and there was nobody else at home.
I said, "I want to go home!"
But he said, "No. We'll go soon.
We'll play a wee game and we'll play music or hide and seek."
I said "No!"
He said, "You can't go home until you play music
or one of these games".
So I said, "hide and seek".
He went upstairs to hide.
I thought I could get out the door, but I couldn't reach the latch.
I was trying to get the latch off the door,
and I heard him calling me,
"If you don't come and get me, you'll never go home!"
There was a big velvet curtain
that hung on the stairs to keep out the draft
and I knew that once I passed the curtain and went up the stairs…*

*Each stair was like forever.
I just put my hand on the handle of the door and that's
where he brought me.*

I kept closing my eyes and saying,

"I want to go home! I want to go home!"
And he said I could go home after
he did what he wanted to do to me.
And he told me not to tell anybody.
Something bad was happening.
Something so dark and scary.
I went into the pretend world where I am always safe.
The world of fairy tales and angels where I can be anybody I want.
Like the Little Mermaid and Cinderella.
I love those beautiful dresses.
I love dolls, and imaginary antique houses
that smell of clean wood and fairies and angels.
I love their wee wings.
In my dreams I can put my arms out and just rise up into the air.
I'm dancing.
Flying free.

A few years ago, I went to a medium,
and my uncle came through her asking me to forgive him.
I couldn't do it.
I told him I had only been eleven
and he'd been an old man who knew what he was doing.
Then I asked him, "Why did you do it to me?"
And he said, "Because I knew you wouldn't say nothing.
You were the quiet one."
And that's what sickened me. I asked myself,
Why can't I speak out?

A while ago I drove up to the top of
the hill in Derry and I saw a light streaming through
the door of the Presbyterian church.
It lit up the whole night. A thought came to me.
If I go in there, could I be cleansed?

Sanctuary

*I was always searching for my mother's love.
I always wanted to know I was safe.*

*Even when I saw her face of fear,
the day she ran to get my Granda
and left us wains alone in the house with shooting all around.
"If I'm not back in ten minutes, you'll know I was shot."
The day guns were put through our front door
and mobs screamed, "We know you're in there, you Fenians!"
The day she ran out to the street and yelled at the violent crowd:
"Take off your masks. I know who you are!"
The day when my daddy told us
they'd given us only a few hours to get out.*

*I clung to her when we all squeezed into that one wee car.
No room for our clothes, nappies, or even my mother's coat.
We made our way to the Holy Child School,
where there were thousands of families
who'd been put out of their homes.*

*I hugged Mammy as close as I could when all six of us
slept on the one mattress on the gymnasium floor,
grey blankets rolled at its feet.
I held her hand as we queued up for food.
Resting my head on her arm, her leg, her chest.*

*I breathed her despair when my aunt told her of
returning to our house
and finding there was nothing left to fetch.
The men had taken our furniture out on the street and set it on fire.
Dancing around it as they laughed and yelled sectarian slogans.*

*I sought my mother's comfort when we fled one falling down house
to another.
Living like refugees.*

*Running from the sounds of soldiers smashing windows
on our walk.
Helicopters.
Shootings.
The smells of burnt tyres, blackened streets and the fire red sky.
When we lived in the republican 'safe house',
where injured men hid guns and bandages
in the room we weren't allowed in.
The houses of broken toilets, falling off wallpaper, holes in the floor.
Dirt.
Stink.*

*I yearned for my mother.
When she had a nervous breakdown and couldn't show her love.
When she disowned me after I got pregnant at age sixteen.
When I went into premature labour at only six months,
after running from gunfire in the streets.
And gave birth to my wee daughter
who only weighed less than two pounds.*

*I wanted my mother to hold me
when I went back and forth to the hospital,
praying for my daughter to live.
When the nurse called and said she'd be dead
in the next ten minutes.
When I held her wee fingers in mine, praying for her to
hold on to life.
When the priest asked me, who did I want to shut the coffin?
And I said "My Daddy".
The first and last time I ever saw him cry.*

*I always wanted my mother's love.
When I ran from abuse, the violence in my marriage.
When I too broke down and tried to kill myself.
When I couldn't get out of the bed, the house, my depression.
When I didn't know my own strength.*

It took me years to find that strength.
It took the love and wisdom of counsellors at a women's refuge,
where they listened to me even when I sat mute for months.
Where they came and got me out of bed.
Where they taught me that I could write, speak,
and be a good mother to my children.
They gave me confidence and helped me through the darkest times.
They nurtured me, cared for me.
Showed me love.

I always wanted to be the mother I never had.
I wanted to be the sanctuary for my children.
Be their strength.

It was 4am, a year and a half ago.
I woke to a phone call from my son's daddy.
"Don't panic. It's Michael.
He's been beaten in an attack and is in intensive care.
They don't know if he'll make it."

I drove from Derry to Belfast, praying for him the whole way down.
When I got to hospital, they told me that he'd died at the scene,
and they revived him.
The next twenty-four hours would be crucial,
and they prepared us for the worst.
I had never seen anything like the way he looked.
Tubes, pipes, bandages.
He wasn't breathing on his own,
and his face was black, blue and purple.
It was swollen out to here.
The breathing machine was going up and down, up and down.
But I felt calm as I put my hands on his heart.
He lay there lifeless.
I know you're in there Michael – you need to fight."
I knew he'd be ok. I just felt it.

The police told us it was a sectarian beating.
Michael had been at a club celebrating with a friend,
when some guys heard his last name.
"McCann."
They jumped his friend and Michael must have
stepped in to save him.
One of them later said,
"If the police hadn't come in, we'd have killed the Fenian bastard!"
It was a vicious beating. Michael ended up with
nineteen plates in his face,
eighty-four stitches on his head, three surgeries,
and he now faces endless treatments.

I spent every day in hospital giving him Reiki,
and praying over him,
until he began to heal.
He had to be resuscitated three times.

I surrounded him with a mother's love and kept
laying my hands on his chest.
I brought all the light and love I could to him.
He was twenty-nine, but he was still my baby and
I had to do everything to keep giving him life.

After the attack, lots of people were really angry,
and wanted revenge.
I had to put out the word:
"I want nothing done. Michael is in there fighting for his life.
I don't want you out there hurting somebody else's son."
I had to plea for peace.

I always wanted my mother's love.
I always wanted to know I was safe.
I always wanted to find my own strength.
I always wanted to become my own sanctuary.

The Place of Sanctuary

It was a just a few years after the tour of *I Once Knew a Girl*, that Therese truly found the place of sanctuary and strength within her. Following the vicious sectarian attack on her son Michael; instead of becoming angry and depressed, Therese sat at his bedside for months, surrounding him with love and healing prayer. Her desire to prevent any other mother from suffering like she was, drove her to plead for non-violence with those who wanted to avenge his attack. The miracle is that somehow, she found that place of refuge, peace and healing within herself, even after experiencing so many traumas in her lifetime.

That journey wasn't easy. Very few people live through the amount of abuse and violence Therese endured. Fewer still emerge, not only intact, but also able to express love so freely. For much of her lifetime, Therese's response to the trauma had been to become mute, depressed and to retreat into her imaginary worlds. But through telling her story in Theatre of Witness' *I Once Knew a Girl*, she began to bloom.

I watched her evolve from the timid silent woman who never spoke, to the performer who eloquently gave voice to all she had once held in secret. To the woman who found the courage to confront the mother of her son's attacker. Her transformation was nothing short of miraculous.

Therese was also part of the cast in *Sanctuary*, the final Theatre of Witness project we did in Northern Ireland. It was performed by people who had lost their homes during the Troubles, refugees who fled from African countries at war, and social workers serving refugees.

Therese's story of the sectarian violence that caused her family's continuous displacement, together with the horrific beating of her son, had eerie similarities to the stories of refugees now trying to create safe lives for themselves in

Northern Ireland. She not only fit in with both groups. She became a mentor to the performers in *Sanctuary*, giving them confidence in their own strength, and helping them deal with their fears and doubts about publicly sharing their stories. She became a safe haven for them; a sanctuary for herself and her son, and a model of peace for all of us.

First Encounter

I first met Therese at a family counselling centre where I was recruiting women to collaborate with us for *I Once Knew A Girl*. Therese didn't speak that day in the group, and I later learned that she had never spoken in group. But during the meeting, our eyes met, and for me, time seemed to stand still. I had the sense that years of stories were trying to break free inside of her, so I invited her to meet with me one-on-one. I hoped that in a private format, she might trust me enough to speak.

> *I was drowning until I met you. My mammy had died, and I had no perspective. I couldn't read and couldn't write, and people called me stupid.*
>
> *That's what I thought I was.*
>
> *I didn't want to live anymore, and I was just hoping for something to happen, because every time I tried to commit suicide, it didn't work. I got a message from the angels saying, "No matter what you do, we're sending you back". I was thinking there's no point to hurting myself or hurting my family, 'cos I'm going to come back again.*
>
> *That turned my life completely around. Nobody ever said that they believed in me or listened to me. I was always the stupid one sitting in the corner. The one who would not do nothing. But then you helped me do this, and I'm not afraid anymore.*
>
> **I was just this flower blooming.**

Relationships of Healing

It was easy to fall in love with Therese. Her fundamental goodness shone through. In the quiet space between us, her stories began to pour out and there was an energy of sacred trust between us. It reminds me that there are no real techniques in Theatre of Witness. Instead, there are Guiding Principles that underpin the process. And one of the most foundational of them is the invitation to fall in love with each performer.

A genuine deep sense of appreciation, curiosity and compassion, encourages participants to open up. It creates the soft landing for when painful memories and emotions emerge. It can't be faked. It comes with authentic presence and love. And it spreads throughout the group, supporting blossoming relationships between participants. When we were working on *Sanctuary*, Therese befriended everyone quickly, taking a leadership position because she had already performed in *I Once Knew a Girl*.

> *I made good friends with Lloyd and Maryama, (from Zimbabwe and Somalia), and the connection I have with them, it's unbelievable. If I hadn't done the play, I wouldn't be able to help people. It's amazing. I can't explain it. Amazing the ripple effects. It helps my kids be strong. My family was all proud of me when I did the two plays.*

Superpower

In the beginning, Therese didn't believe she was smart. But when listening to her, I saw a bright and intuitive woman who trusted her own potent medicine of beauty and imagination. In our individual sessions, when she focused her attention on the world of angels or fairies, it transformed her whole nervous system. So, I decided to alternate our sessions; between inviting her to delve into the stories about the abusive and violent times of her life, with sessions of dance, drawing and music. This helped her to stay emotionally steady.

Past therapists had tried to turn Therese away from 'escaping' into that magic place where she found her safe haven. They felt it was important to ground her in reality. But I saw that Therese's genuine love of beauty, mystical realms and joyous expression was actually her medicine.

She continued to do the hard work of confronting her raw, yet invisible, wounds with incredible courage. But that darkness was now balanced with forays into creative expression and visualisations that brought her joy and love. I didn't know many people who had suffered the degree of trauma Therese had, who still retained that childlike capacity for love and joy. To me, that was the key to her strength and her superpower. It just needed to be appreciated and nurtured.

Through our sessions, our mutual love continued to grow. Therese trusted me, and I trusted that beautiful place of refuge inside of her. Our personal connection helped to smooth the way for her to slowly open up to the other women in our group. Our circle became a safe place of listening and empathy, where every woman's hidden stories were cherished. She thrived.

But at the beginning, when she first told her story to the other performers, she was scared.

> *I waited to be the last person to speak. I wondered whether the women would believe me. It took my breath away that they did, because all my life people didn't. When I saw that they believed me, it gave me belief in myself.*
>
> **It opened my heart and soul.**

Unlocking Secrets

It takes strength to disclose memories that have been locked up for years in shame. As Therese began to believe in her own strength, she shared some of the stories in the group, and later, onstage. But the stigma and secrecy of sexual abuse is so pervasive; it's no surprise that Therese's first assumption would be that the other women wouldn't believe her. It took all of her courage to speak about incest and sexual abuse to others.

But instead of being judged, Therese's stories opened the door for the other women to reveal their own experiences with sexual violence. It helped to bond the group. And it helped Therese believe in her own strength.

However, it required another level of bravery to speak of these shocking familial stories in front of her family at public performances. It was the first time they heard of the abuse.

> *My younger brother came over and he hugged me, and he says, "I believe you. Why didn't you tell us? We would have protected you." But I was only six years old and who would have believed me then? He said, "All your life you were abused, but you never said nothing".*
>
> *I was told not to say nothing. I just carried it. But now I'm not afraid. If someone asks me a question after seeing the film, I'll be honest about it.*

Holding Up the Mirror

When I develop a performer's script, one of my goals is to reflect back to them their own positive qualities which they perhaps have not yet acknowledged. Sometimes when writing their parts, I take a few liberties, and include something they may have intimated but didn't exactly say. Of course, we then discuss it, and the performer decides if they feel comfortable adding it to their part. I did this when I wrote the last stanza of the poem for Therese that she presented in *I Once Knew a Girl*.

> "But I once knew a girl who grew into her strength.
> Who learned to say NO, and claimed her own life.
> Who never stopped imagining,
> even when her world was dark.
> Who got help and support and found she wasn't alone.
> I am that girl. Therese Parker McCann.
> A woman of strength!"
>
> That poem made me who I am.
> I say it to myself all the time even now, twelve years later.
>
> Teya reached inside my soul and took my words and put it into the production. Things hiding inside of me that I couldn't get out. She made me believe in myself.
>
> **I actually believe I am a woman of strength now.**

That courage Therese now feels touches all aspects of her life.

> When Michael got beat up, I didn't want no retaliation. I went to court that day and I saw the mother. She was sitting there crying. I was so angry. When the judge was saying about how they beat that young fellow to death, I said I had to say something. I wasn't cheeky or nothing, but I went over to the mother and said, "Excuse me, but I'm Michael's mother, the one that your son just beat up".
>
> And she says, "Well, I'm really sorry for what he's done. But he's getting punished for it now. He's not like that."
>
> I said, "But my son's left disabled for the rest of his life". I don't know where I got that courage from, because I've never, ever done that in my life. I just needed to get that out and let her know that I was the mother of the one that they beat up.

But healing comes in stages and cycles. There is no miracle pill or process that makes fears go away. There is only intention and support.

> *I've faced my fears about my uncle Robert. I feel strong. I don't feel scared. But when I see my cousin, it makes me sick to my stomach. I don't know what to do. But maybe the universe will take care of him. I don't have the courage to face him. I want to get stronger to get rid of that fear.*
>
> *I kept that secret all my life, because I just thought they'd blame me and say, "You're telling lies". I wished that I would have had the strength, but it wasn't the time. And obviously, I wasn't meant to do this, until now. Anyway, God finally gave me a voice.*

The Quiet Voice

The longer I do this work, the more I realise that it is sometimes the quiet voices which speak the loudest. During the Troubles, it was the voices of men which were heard and acknowledged. Voices of women and girls, especially those talking about abuse or women's issues, were totally disregarded. That is certainly true for Therese.

She has a speaking voice once accustomed to being silenced and overlooked. But Therese's story is one that many other girls and women recognise and identify with. Now when she speaks, there is also an inner strength of moral conviction that comes through in her tone and words. One can hear her own transformation from meekness to strength. It is a voice that inspires.

> *As a child, and then as a teen and adult woman, I never thought I'd ever be where I am today, speaking and helping people. I love it to bits.*
>
> *I'm not a brilliant speaker. But I know I have healing, and I can help people.*
>
> *When I go into schools and tell them about my life, and about the abuse and Troubles, they listen.*

> *If I can give courage to one woman who was abused, then I am happy.*

> *When we performed in Enniskillen, people were coming over to talk to me afterwards about my sharing about the abuse I went through. This woman came over to me and says, "I'm going to tell you something. This happened to me, and I've never told anybody. This is the first time. I am going to go get help." And I thought, oh my God!*

> *We did a workshop in a school, and this young girl of about fifteen started asking me more details. She said, "That happened to me". She'd already told the school and was getting support, but she wanted to see how I was able to cope with it, and how I got through it. I told her all the things that happened to me and how I was able to talk about it. So I've made her more confident to talk about it too.*

> **The biggest thing in my life is my voice now, and the courage that I have been given.**

Many of us think of peace as something large, like a governmental agreement, a treatise by experts, or the absence of violence. But there is another kind of peace being created in homes and schools and families. It is a much more subtle and quiet peace. It listens to the voices of children and acknowledges the psychological impact of abuse, bullying, and violence. The kind of peace that one person feels in the presence of another. It is based on love and caring and understanding. Therese embodies this peace and has, in the aftermath of years of war, dislocation, poverty and hatred, become a quiet example of peace as healing. Peace as sanctuary.

> *I always wanted to become a sanctuary for my own children.*

Ordinary Woman

Anne Walker

Ordinary Woman in Extraordinary Circumstances

I used to love this country.
How do you love yourself and your country at the same time?

My mammy's brother was shot to death on Bloody Sunday.
I was three years old, and we all flew home from Wales.
I remember the air hostess giving me and my sister Michelle sheets
of plastic paper to play with that had sets of eyes and noses and
mouths that you could change to make up different faces.
And when we got to me granny's house in the Bogside,
I remember the house being full of people lining the stairs.
And then after that, everything was about the Troubles.
Everything.
Life was getting stopped and searched, news bulletins,
Bloody Sunday marches every year.
Bombs.
Shootings.
Seeing the Provos' shows of strength.
Our house was raided a lot in the early mornings.
One time Daddy was taken off and arrested.
And one time Mam was arrested.

We lived by the news.
You got up in the morning and the television and radio came on
with the news.
You came home from school at lunch
and the television and radio were on with the news.
No matter what was going on in the whole world,
6pm was time for news.
I absorbed it all.
At age nine at school we made Easter cards.
Mine had a picture of Mam and Dad, a dead body and guns.

I used to go to stay at my granny's a lot,
and she and I always talked about how we'd sort the country out.
We were always on the right side doing the right thing
and everyone else was doing it wrong.
The Brits and police had us terrorised.
I knew lots of people that had been killed by the Brits and the police.
She talked about her son who was killed on Bloody Sunday
with great pride.
My granny was great. She liked to stay up late,
and she fed you toast.
When you were in bed, she threw holy water over you.
My granny was a great hero, because even though
there were loads of kids and loads of grandchildren,
nothing ever fazed her.
She was always ready to chat. Always ready to listen.
She was always lovely.

When I stayed over at her house, and I knew
there was trouble in the town,
I would climb out the return window, jump on the top of the shed,
jump down, run down the lane down the town,
sit on the walls and watch the riots.
The first time I did it, I thought, how will I get back in again?
I did that a whole lot of times,
getting back into bed about five or six,

Then up at seven, dressed, and over to my mammy's house,
and out to school.

When I was twelve, I went out with an eighteen-year-old.
It was wrong, but it didn't feel wrong enough.
He showed me a gun when I was thirteen and it was exciting.
I thought, Oh my God! I want to be a part of this!
I want to save Ireland!
I wanted to save everybody.
It was a dream.
It was an ideal.
I never said no.

When I was thirteen,
I acted and looked far older than I should have.
I fancied all the boys who were running around in balaclavas
and throwing petrol bombs.
The IRA were our saviours, our heroes, our protectors.
In my eyes, they could do no wrong.
At age thirteen, the Hunger Strikes sealed my fate.
I became so republican and fired up,
that I could have told you the names and times of death
of each of the hunger strikers.

When I was fourteen, there was an election,
and I impersonated people at election places for Sinn Fein.
At one place I used a Protestant name, and when it was called out,
another woman said she was there for that family.
I had to walk out in front of the police.
But I got fourteen votes that day.

I felt like a heroine, but I hated the lying.
I got good at secrets and hiding.
I felt empowered but guilty.
Every which way but loose.

*I remember going to confession and saying the same sins
over and over again every week.
I remember promising not to do them again,
and coming back and saying the same sins and wondering,
how are you supposed to get through a week
without doing anything wrong?
It was hard to be a Catholic and harbour the thoughts and feelings
I was having.*

*Most people who want to become combatants go looking to be.
But I was asked.
I was eighteen and a fellow I knew well stopped me one day
and said something to the effect about joining the IRA,
and I said, "I don't know how you could join the IRA.
I wouldn't even know who to ask. Why are you asking me?"
And he says, "I'm not asking you to help me join.
I'm asking you to join up."*

*And, to tell you the truth, I got such a rush
that he felt that I was good enough
and had something to offer more than going on
marches and demonstrations,
that I said, "I don't need to think about it.
I know what I want to do."
I'd always felt, that because I was a girl, nobody would want me.
So that day when that fellow asked me to join up,
I was on Cloud Nine.
Somebody wants me for something now,
and what better cause to be in, than the one that's making us free?
I felt important. They needed me.
It all seemed like a very, very exciting life for me.*

*It wasn't long after joining that I was assigned to
be a quartermaster in charge of moving guns and explosives.
It was a bit like being in sales,
and I've been a salesperson and I was good at it.* |

*You had to sell people on the idea of agreeing to
conduct meetings in their house, or to store guns, or explosives.
I travelled up and down the country in buses moving gear around.*

*I once travelled on a bus with a handgun down my trousers
that I was delivering to a house in Derry.
There was a fellow in the back of the bus chatting me up,
and I was thinking that if I didn't have this gun down my trousers,
I would probably go for it 'cos he was really nice.
I ended up with this massive gun-shaped bruise
from carrying the gun around all day.
I can't remember what I did with the gun,
but I ended up getting rid of it and going home late
and lying again.
It's all about lying.*

*It all felt brilliant, but I hated the lying.
If my mam and dad had found out what I was doing,
it would have killed them.
But it was exciting, and I lived on adrenaline.
When you live on adrenaline, reality is a deep hole to fall into.*

*There are some funny stories from that time.
I was with a crowd at a safe house one night
getting weapons training.
It was Christmas time and freezing outside.
We were being taught how to strip weapons,
and the next thing we knew,
the place filled up with Saracens and Brits.
They were everywhere.
We all thought: Right, that is it. There's going to be a shoot-out.
There's going to be people dead.
We put all the lights out. We were sitting with our weapons,
shaking but ready.*

I remember looking down at the doorway.

And then a knock came to the door and all we heard was
"We wish you a merry Christmas,
we wish you a merry Christmas, we…"
It was flippin' carol singers!
We all started giggling with a big sigh of relief.
The big man really looks after me, he does.

Another time we were in this house
and there was a knock at the front door,
and it was obvious to us that the RUC had come into the house.
I was in the kitchen, with this other guy who was quite high up.
We were two people they would have loved to have lifted.
And we were very quiet and I said to him,
"If they come in here, I'll be jumping on your knees and kissing you,
'cos I don't want them thinking that
it's anything other than romance".
Recently I heard someone talk about that night,
and they said that he told them that I did sit on his knees
and did kiss him.
It's funny after all these years to find out how the story is told.
Some stories just sound better than the truth.

It's hard to be a woman combatant.
You have to prove that you're up there with them.
You have to never say no, and always do what you're supposed to do,
and not let yourself or them down.
Even though I was terrified and unconfident when they said,
"This is what we want you to do",
I always said, "No problem".
And I might have stood in front of them and said, "No problem",
but would have walked out the door and thought,
How the 'F' am I going to do this?
You end up overdoing it and they think you're brilliant,
as you try to prove that you can do whatever they can do.

So you do the utmost, so they can't say,
"She's a woman; she can't do it".

And you end up in a situation where
they think you can do everything.

At one stage I was a unit leader.
There were four men under me and I was their boss.
And I wondered: How in the world did this happen to me?
How am I going to get four men to do what I'm telling them to do?
And I never ever knew if I got that position
because I was good enough
or because of my boss.
He came on so strong and pressured me sexually a few times,
and in that situation there is no one to turn to.
Nobody to talk to.
He was the big boss.
The affair wasn't something that I wanted,
but I was a soldier.
I didn't know how to say no to people.
People with power and authority used to have me, like that!
And who would have believed me?
It was very hard to deal with,
because on top of lying to my family and boyfriend
about where I was,
there was that thing going on as well,
I didn't know how to stop it.

But one particular day I was called to man an explosive device
that the British army was guaranteed to go past.
That day I had a sore head.
I knew I didn't want to do it, not 'cos my head was sore,
but because I had been running guns,
and I hadn't ever been directly involved in having to kill somebody.
And that night I was going to be directly involved
in watching people getting blown up.

When I went down to meet up with the other fellow
who was going to be with me on this job,

*I was glad it was going to be him,
'cos he was one of the good guys and he treated me like a friend.
He treated me like one of the boys
and not like a woman in the sexual sense.*

*When I was with him and waiting for the patrol to go past,
I really badly had to go to the toilet.
There was a pub close by and he said,
You better go. I don't want any accidents here."
So I said, "I'll be back in two seconds".
and went to the pub and went to the bathroom.*

*And when I came out, there were steps for me to run up,
and when I ran up the steps,
it felt as if someone had hit me in the head with a hammer.
There was a God-awful pain in my head,
and I ran around to him and
I took one look at him.
And he said, "What happened to you?"
I said, "I don't feel so good".
He said, "Go home".
And I said, "I'm not leaving you. I'll stay here."
He said, "You have to go. You look terrible."
I says, "No, I'll stay, I'll stay".
And within the next couple of minutes
I started throwing my guts up.
He made me go, and he said,
"Don't worry about this. I'll get in touch with them.
Get you off and away. There's no sign of them coming anyway."
And he made me go home.*

*It transpired that I'd had a brain haemorrhage.
I ended up needing full brain surgery.
My daddy held my hand all night long
watching me throw up blood,
not knowing if I'd live or die.*

*The life I was leading could have left me close to death
by bombs, bullets or life imprisonment,
and how hard would it have been for my daddy to
hold my hand then?*

*I believe God works in mysterious ways.
That was one hell of a mysterious way
to get me out of that situation.
It turns out that the Brits were
never gonna' come that night anyway,
thank God,
because an informer had informed on the whole thing.
But what would have happened that night,
was that if we had been around any longer,
they would have picked us up
and that would have been the end of us.
We would have been doing time or maybe even be dead.
But the Brits weren't ever going to come that night. And I'm glad.
That's not what I was supposed to be doing.
It's not even what I wanted to be doing.
I wanted to be part of the cause,
I wanted to be part of the justice of setting Ireland free.
I wanted to be part of the dream and I had seen so much,
but it was never in me to go so far down that road.
It was never in me to be that type of person.
Is it really in anybody?*

*I believe God said, "Anne, you won't stop yourself. I'll stop you."
I would have come so close to pressing the button
and blowing soldiers into smithereens
and lived the rest of my life thinking of their mothers, daughters.
I never would have lived with myself.
After the brain haemorrhage, that informer got us all arrested.*

*My mother is one of the strongest people I know.
She even convinced me that I would be OK*

when I had the haemorrhage,
and I believed her and wasn't afraid.
But she completely fell apart the morning they arrested me.
She knew how wrong it could have gone.

A load of us who were in the same team were taken to Castlereagh.
I was in there for two days.
I began to get interrogated by two policemen
and they started with the usual, "Name. Address."
And I began thinking: What am I doing here?
I wonder what it is they think I've done?
Because I couldn't work out what they would have known.
And I put my feet up on the pipe and I was trying to act real cool,
closing my arms, putting my feet up, thinking:
This is the start of it, now I'm going to get it.
So the policeman says,
"So you think you're a big girl now, don't you?"
I didn't say anything.
I needed to hear what they thought they had on me.
"Beating up a security guard, blowing up a tax office,
you think you're a big girl."
I thought: I didn't do that. Happy days, I'll be out in a few days.
I didn't know where the tax office was.
I wouldn't have beat anyone up.
That's not nice.
This is the dilemma.
I was a good girl. And I was a nice girl. And I was a sweetheart.
And I tried my best to be a good girl.
But at the same time there was a war going on.
It was mental.
Then the police told me that they were sending me out,
and I actually said,
"No, I'm not going anywhere".
They said, "No, no, you're really getting out".
And I tried to hold onto the bed.
I didn't want them to take me out,
'cos I thought if they took me out after two days,

the Provos would think I was informing and I'd get shot.
They're supposed to keep you five days or something.
I was terrified of coming out.
I was terrified of going in,
but I was actually terrified of coming out.
I thought: You can't do this to me.

I never said, "That's me, I'm out",
and they never said, "That's you, you're gone".
But a few months after being in hospital,
my involvement with the IRA just dissipated.
But I missed the adrenaline high.
I needed something to replace it.
So I went down the drug road and danced
my wee heart out at clubs.
I replaced one high with another with another and another.

After Castlereagh, the personal harassment became unbearable.
I looked for an out from drugs, family and harassment,
and moved to Limerick, where I met a man and got married.

Me and my ex-husband, we get on alright now,
but he broke me in ways that the police and the Brits couldn't.
I went through the Troubles on these streets,
and the Brits and police crucified me,
but my husband broke me in ways…
He should have been a flippin' RUC man, I swear to God.

I had always had it in my head that if a man hit me,
I would hit back no matter what.

The first time he hit me, I hit him back.
And the next time I hit him, he fell to the floor.
I remember looking at his head thinking,
Don't hit him Anne, 'cos you'll really hurt him.
And I kicked him anyway. I thought I could handle it.

I suppose I thought: I used to be in the IRA,
I don't have to take this.
I'll just hit him back.
I became what I didn't want to be.

None of us were taught how to be a woman properly.
The boys weren't taught how to be proper men.
A lot of the men who were my heroes
ended up being violent with women.
Maybe some of it was caused by the frustration of
not being able to talk about the Troubles.
Maybe it was about fighting for power.
It's the damage of war and a culture
that doesn't get talked about here.
I've worked hard now to control myself and to forgive my ex.
I forgive him every day.

It took me a long time to realise that the people I'd held up high
as the heroes weren't the heroes I thought they were.
Over the years the disillusionment has grown
and grown and grown.
I now think we did it all wrong.
But then, I didn't know any better.
I didn't see the bigger picture.
And I didn't look to the future to see what could possibly happen.
When I look back at it all now, because I was a quartermaster,
moving things around the country,
I probably was directly involved in getting people killed.
That's real hard to take.
I want to learn to forgive myself.

The biggest job I have now is to be the best mother I can be to Asa.
I want to ensure that he'll grow up and be
a healthy, mature grown man
who doesn't get caught up in it all.
We've been gardening at our allotment together.

He's learning the fiddle.
I've done some courses in photography
and am channelling my energy into creativity.
I'm finally learning to follow my own dreams.

Everybody is ordinary.
We just end up in extraordinary circumstances.

I Do Have a Story

> **Part of my role as a peacemaker, truthteller,**
> **and taboo breaker, is not to hide in shame anymore.**

Anne recently wrote the following for a presentation:

> *'When we began this journey years ago,*
> *I didn't think I had a story.*
> *Later, I didn't yet know the Anne*
> *who was bigger than that story.*
>
> *I'm not just Anne from the IRA.*
> *Not just the wee Catholic girl who grew up on the Bogside,*
> *Whose uncle was killed on Bloody Sunday.*
> *Not just Anne who went through*
> *a messy marriage and divorce.*
> *Who had a brain haemorrhage.*
> *Who lived through abuse and rape.*
>
> *I'm Anne who is grateful to have transformed*
> *her brokenness to resilience.*
> *The mother, daughter, sister.*
> *Friends with ex-police, ex-opposing combatants, ex-army,*
> *victims and survivors even ex white supremacists.*
> *I'm Anne who will be working with gender-based violence*
> *across the world.*
> *Who loves the natural way.*
> *The visionary.*

*I'm Anne who is not afraid to say the things
that others are afraid to say*

When we began this journey, I didn't think I had a story...'

Beginning the Process

When I was recruiting for performers for *I Once Knew a Girl*, I wanted to find at least one female ex-combatant. A month before, Kathleen Gillespie, whose husband Patsy had been horrifically murdered by the IRA at Coshquin, had asked to be in the project. She had come to our first production where Robin, a serving police officer, had shared his story about being on the Body Recovery Team after the Coshquin bomb. She had been very moved and asked if she could be in the next production.

So I knew that whoever I added to this new group of performers would need to be able to match Kathleen's strength, fortitude and courage. The ex-combatant would also need to be someone who truly believed in peace. And able to deeply and honestly empathise with the grief and anger Kathleen felt, while at the same time, attending to the truth and trajectory of her own story.

Anne was recommended to me by a former republican ex-combatant who was deeply involved in peace dialogues. All I knew from him was that Anne had been a member of the IRA and that she had a powerful story.

At our first one-on-one meetings, Anne cried continually. In trying to discern whether she was far enough past the traumas she'd experienced to safely 'witness' them without emotional harm, I went back to my contact. He was certain she was strong enough and that the emotional distress she was expressing now was a necessary part of her healing process and essential to the work we'd be doing. Right away I saw Anne had a fierce determination.

> *In my original interviews with Teya, my body cried it all out. She wasn't sure whether I was strong enough to do the project. When she showed me some of the videos of the projects that she'd done in America, something happened to me. I saw the power of the work. And that was further enhanced when I saw the 'We Carried Your Secrets' documentary film.*
>
> *I remember that night going, "I'm gonna be in this. I'm gonna do whatever I can to be a part of this." And it wasn't because I wanted fame or notoriety, or even to tell my story, but I could see the power of the work from way back then. And maybe that's why I'm so passionate now about how we go forward.*

Anne put her finger on one of the most important characteristics that I look for when choosing performers. I want to work with people who desire to tell their stories, not for their own self-satisfaction or because they love to perform, but because they hope their story may be helpful to someone else. That want to take the pain of one's own life experience and willingly reopen the wound so that it can benefit others, is a brave and powerful quality.

Bravery

Although the tears were plentiful, I saw in Anne an indescribable courage. A willingness to peel back the layers of her story and really dig in.

> *The more I visit the pain, the more I heal, and other people can relate. I want to bring people out of their dark shame.*

That fearlessness was also evident in her willingness to openly tell her story about having been a quartermaster in the IRA

- a story that could potentially land her in jail, as historical inquiries were still going on, and she had never before been convicted for being part of an illegal organisation. There was also potential danger to her safety from current republican dissidents who might not want her telling her story publicly.

It also took a remarkable amount of emotional courage for her to disclose her experiences about active involvement in the IRA in front of Kathleen, who had been made a widow by that organisation.

Relationship Building

When we first brought the group of participants together for *I Once Knew a Girl*, everyone was apprehensive. But none more than Kathleen and Anne. Each knew about the other and both feared that it might be excruciatingly painful to listen to the other's stories. They also weren't sure how each of them would be received. Would Anne be able to deeply empathise with Kathleen's grief and anger without defensiveness? Would Kathleen be open to understanding what had led Anne to join the IRA? I don't think either of them slept the night before.

> *When I went into the room and seen Kathleen, I nodded at her and she nodded back. I was physically shaking. Physically shaking, and close to tears and thinking: Right, how is this going to go?*
> Anne from The Far Side of Revenge documentary, by Margo Harkin

Listening in a Safe Circle

We began as we always did, by sitting in a circle. As part of this ritual, I rang the bell and we sat for a minute in silence; each of us going inward to discern what positive gift we were bringing to the group before sharing one by one. Then we started with the women relating their stories in any order they chose.

Kathleen volunteered to go first. But somehow, I knew that if she did, it would have been almost impossible emotionally for Anne to follow. So I suggested Anne tell her story first.

> *By the end of me telling these women what I could of me story, the tears were running down my cheeks. And I turned around to Kathleen, and she put her arms around me and she gave me a big hug. And she cried, and I cried. And I thanked her, and she told me it was OK. And I couldn't believe it. The last thing I expected that day was her reaction.*
> **From The Far Side of Revenge**

When I spoke to Anne twelve years later about the intense friendship she and Kathleen have developed, she told me it all unfolded from that very first meeting.

> *It wasn't about forgiveness. It was the grace that Kathleen showed me that day that set us up for our journey.*

That grace didn't come all at once. Kathleen had previously done years of intense peace work with ex-combatant groups at Glencree that helped lay the foundation for her to be open and gracious to Anne. Thus unlocking the potential for friendship. The closeness these two women have now is like a jewel, as Kathleen has expressed in her chapter.

Family Ripple Effects

When we began writing Anne's part, she realised that she couldn't tell her family what she was going to say onstage. They didn't know she had been in the IRA, and Anne was terrified of their reaction. She also wanted to protect them from knowing about the sexual abuse and domestic violence she had experienced.

> *Mammy and Daddy did not want me to do the Theatre of Witness production. And they didn't come to see it. The night of the very first performance when everybody else's families were there to congratulate them, I was standing at the end of the stage, quite brilliantly happy with the performance, but conscious that there was nobody there for me.*

While Anne's parents weren't present to honour her; surprisingly, it was the family of cast member Catherine McCartney from a Protestant loyalist community in Belfast who first reached out and congratulated her. For them to show respect and care to a woman who had been part of the IRA was a significant gesture, and a testament to how the production had opened their hearts.

> *Catherine's whole family all came up to me one by one and gave me handshakes and hugs. It made me conscious that night that where my own mammy and daddy were coming from was fear.*

The production of *I Once Knew a Girl* toured through 2011. Two years later, filmmaker Margo Harkin's documentary, *The Far Side of Revenge*, which followed the performers and their relationships in creating and touring the project, debuted. It was then broadcast on BBC TV.

> *'The Far Side of Revenge' came on TV, and I remember saying to my parents: "Don't be channel-surfing tonight because the documentary I was in will be on TV".*
>
> *The next day when I went to their house, my mammy was sitting in her armchair with her arms folded. She turned around and she says, "I watched that last night you know". And I remember thinking, oh my God, I'm in trouble, and bracing myself. I was expecting her to say "Are you effing stupid? What are you playing at?"*
>
> *But the next words that my mammy actually did say, changed me and my mammy's relationship.*
>
> *"I didn't protect you."*

> *I remember that feeling of relief and thinking, oh my God, is this really my mother saying this? It was a moment of vulnerability which showed more strength than I had seen ever coming from her, and she was a strong woman. But we were able to have conversations after that, which changed how she felt about me getting involved with Theatre of Witness and telling my truths.*
>
> *I was finally able to recognise vulnerability in my own mammy.*
>
> *As a result of that, she became one of my biggest supporters right up until the day she died.*
>
> *She even got around to having Theatre of Witness performers in her home. People she absolutely would never have let come in: police, soldiers, ex-UDA. She went on to have incredible pride for the strength that I have, instead of worrying and being fearful for me. I knew that I had done the right thing. I knew it anyway.*
>
> **Those four words, "I didn't protect you", changed everything.**

When Anne's mother died, the family had a ceremony following the cremation. Anne told her siblings and extended family the story about what her mother had said to her and the great healing they shared. Then she added that she recounts this moment at all workshops.

> *I get to say this about our mammy, all the time, every workshop all over the world. For them, it was learning something new about their mammy, as well as hearing about the workshops.*
>
> *I told them that telling that story at workshops means that I can carry that part of mammy's story with me. It was really emotional.*

What Do We Pass From One Generation to the Next?

Anne's son Asa is also part of the ripple effect. He was ten years old when Anne began creating *I Once Knew a Girl*. Already she was worried about him being recruited by dissident groups. Part of her motivation to speak out was to pave a path of peace for Asa, so he didn't follow his peers into anti-social behaviour.

> *I was completely honest with him when I got involved in Theatre of Witness. I wanted him to be able to ask questions, and I didn't want to be sneaking out and doing stuff.*
>
> *Because I had been in the IRA, my son Asa would have been ripe for the plucking.*
>
> *When he was twelve, he came home one day and he said, "Why aren't you in the IRA anymore?" He told me that all of his friend's dads were in the Dissies (Dissident Republican Groups) and he didn't have anything to brag about. He couldn't tell them that I had been in the IRA.*
>
> *I sat him down and I talked about Theatre of Witness, peace and reconciliation and the people that we were meeting in the workshops. I brought him to see 'Release' (the Theatre of Witness production which followed mine), and he was greatly influenced by all the stories, especially from the police and soldier.*
>
> *Asa now has a group of friends from all different backgrounds, and they recently came to one of our Theatre of Witness workshops and asked me to organise a workshop for their extended friends. They're not a community group and they're not a school; they're just a group of kids who want to know what it is that Asa and Asa's mammy are involved in. They want to be part of it.*
>
> *When I was growing up, I was so impacted by everything*

that was going on around me that I ended up joining the IRA. I wonder if, because Asa has had such across-the-board conversations and met people from so many sides, that he is anti-war, believing that peace works?

The Body Knows

Two years after *I Once Knew a Girl* finished touring, Anne attended Theatre of Witness' *Release*, performed by a group of men who had been involved in the Troubles. The experience was even more immersive and challenging than she had anticipated. But healing too.

> *I remember being in the audience. William, the prison governor, came onstage. I didn't consciously go: I'm not gonna like this person. But my body did. I could feel the hairs in the back of my neck standing up, and I could feel myself physically twisting away. And I was saying to myself: You know the process, you know the story; you've been and done this one.*
>
> *But I was saying to myself, to me: What's wrong? What's wrong? And maybe it was the H-Blocks and the hunger strikes that triggered it all. It wasn't hate. It was just was as if my body triggered into: Right, you can take nearly everything, but this one's difficult.*
>
> *Of all the people who could have walked on that stage; somebody who had been in charge of the Maze prison. And then the penny dropped. I realised that when I walked out on stage, there probably were people in the audience feeling like I was towards William. Some people would find it difficult to accept my story. And that's what Kathleen and Catherine McCartney were probably worried about every time I performed. That some people would find it difficult to accept my story.*
>
> *And that was a massive revelation. And I actually searched*

William out after that performance, because by the end of the story, I had come round. It reconciled me. My body told me, and I talked to him about that, since we are quite good friends and we work well together.

Imagine that if we were able to help perpetrators and watch their journey of healing. Would that be also healing for those who were on the other side of it?

Owning the Perpetrator

Anne recently wrote these words:

I know doubt. I know worthlessness. I know fear. I know grief. I know persecution. I know intimidation. I know discrimination. I know oppression. I know loss. I know bullying. I know humiliation. I know degradation. I know silence. I know abuse. I know rape. I know sexual harassment. I know sadness. I know what broken-hearted means. I know anger. I know poverty. I know hunger. I know failure. I know listening. I know worry. I know anxiety. I know stress. I know depression. I know not wanting to live. I know PTSD. I know years of PTSD.

I realised that I could change some of these words to "I have caused..." or, "How have I caused?" Taking responsibility felt like the truth. And it felt like honesty. I think that's when I realised that I can't be pointing the fingers, when I've done them as well. If I take responsibility out loud, somebody else might too. And that will cause a ripple effect.

That's what we do in Theatre of Witness.
We break the taboos.
If we can break the taboos, others might go forward.
There's a tribe in Africa where if somebody in the village is

doing something wrong, the whole village gets together and sits around and asks, "What is it? What's breaking? What's wrong? What's not right your life? How can we help?" The whole village comes together to get the person back on the right path. And we've lost that. Over generations and generations, we've lost that, but maybe we can do it if we say the truth.

I'm in the truth game.

I don't think I can lie anymore. I used to be a very good liar. I didn't like lying, but I'd lie to protect, I'd lie to keep secrets, I'd lie to stop my mammy from badgering me.

Now I realise that I'm in this peace work for the long haul and it's my passion. And there's no point in going at it half-baked. If I'm doing this, then it's full throttle on open access. The good with the bad. I'm married to it!

May He Be
an Instrument of
Thy Peace

Kathleen Gillespie

The following letters were read by cast members
in Kathleen's part:

Letters

"*Dear Mrs. Gillespie,*
May God bless you all always, but especially at these sad times."
Dublin

"*Dear Gillespie family,*
I was greatly saddened and outraged to hear
that several people had been killed in a bomb explosion
during the night.
I was further distressed to hear of the particularly barbaric manner
in which Mr. Gillespie was murdered.
It was a most dreadful and obscene crime and

I'm sure that the sorrow which you experience
must be almost unbearable.

I have prayed for the repose of Mr. Gillespie's soul
and for all your intentions...
With my sympathy and prayers."
John, age 17

"Dear Mrs. Gillespie and family,
I have never written to anyone before like this,
but I wanted to let you know that there are people worldwide
who feel for you and focus their love on you.
Having seen the horror of what the IRA have done,
we wish to send you our condolences and wishes.
Mr. Gillespie has not died in vain – one day there will be peace.
Our father's family was killed
in the Treblinka concentration camp in 1934."
A sympathiser – Australia

"Dear Kathleen,
Please accept my heartfelt sympathy at your time of great loss.
No words can express how my heart feels for you,
as my husband was murdered this year in front of our two young
sons aged eight and five.
So like yourself and your three children,
our three children and myself are totally devastated and
don't know how to carry on.
I have found that people on both sides of the
community really do care,
and like you and me, cannot understand
why men like Patsy and my husband,
who are innocent family men,
end up as victims.
There are so many questions and no answers."
Northern Ireland

Kathleen

Growing up, my biggest dream,
was to get married and create a home and family.
I met Patsy when I was sixteen.
He offered me a lift and that was that.
We were engaged at seventeen and married at twenty.
He was slow getting to the altar!

Fifteen months after we were married, our first son was born.
He was a full-term stillbirth. We were devastated.
But very quickly we had two more sons, fourteen months apart.
But I got quite ill with the pregnancies
and was told by the doctor not to get pregnant again.
Patsy wanted us to stop, because I was risking my life.
But I knew he craved a daughter, and I loved him so much,
that I was willing to risk anything
to give him the daughter he wanted.
So, we had Jennifer.
You'd have thought no one else had ever had a daughter,
the way he'd parade her around.
Even her two brothers spoiled her.
At last, all of my dreams had come true.

Patsy wasn't involved in anything to do with the Troubles.
But he became a target for the paramilitaries because of his work.
After his own business running a mobile fruit and vegetables van
stopped making money,
he took a job as a civilian worker in the kitchen at Fort George.
The paramilitaries were putting warnings in the paper,
but there weren't other jobs available to unskilled labour.
And Patsy was just trying to support his family.
It restricted our social life quite a lot.
You didn't go out and say you worked for the army.
But they liked him there and Patsy got on well with everyone.

The first trouble was in 1986 when our house
was taken over by the IRA.

The kidnappers stayed in the house with me and the children.
I was terrified, but I had to keep it together for the kids.
Jennifer was only eight.
Patsy was forced to drive our car to the army base
loaded down with two hundred pounds of explosives.
That time he was able to jump out and shout
that the car was loaded.
They did a controlled explosion and he got home around 6am.
After that, the Ministry of Defence said they'd move us anywhere
we wanted, but Patsy was adamant.
"No one will put me out of my home!"

We thought that lightning couldn't strike twice.
But it's not true.
Four years later they eventually succeeded in killing Patsy.

The night before the tragedy,
we spoke to our eldest son Patrick in England
who was going to be celebrating his eighteenth birthday
the next day.
His workmates were taking him out on a pub crawl after work.
The last words Patsy said to him were: "Don't get too drunk, son".
The next night before we went out,
Patsy washed the mahogany kitchen cupboards
with vinegar and water.
He took off his wedding ring and, as usual,
put it on the windowsill.
We left about ten o'clock to visit our friends,
leaving Jennifer at home waiting for Kieran
who was expected shortly.

When we drove back to the house, things didn't look normal.
The hall was dark. There was a key stuck in the front door.

Walking in, I felt a gun to my neck.
I thought it was Kieran playing with me.
"That's not funny, son."

There were two masked men with the guns running down the hall,
more in other places.
I heard Jennifer crying in the sitting room.

They took turns guarding us and
eventually took Patsy away at midnight.
They let him say goodbye to us.
"It will be alright, girl. I'll be home soon."
Since we'd been through this before,
I think we both thought it would be the same thing.

I kept asking questions of the man guarding me in the sitting room.
But all he said was,
"If you do what you are told, everybody will be ok".
And I was stupid enough to believe him.
I wasn't intimidated though.
When I asked permission to use the toilet in my own house,
one of the men came with me.
When he tried to follow me in, I grabbed him and said,
"I'm too fat to get out the window and there's no phone here,
so get out!"

At around five minutes to four o'clock in the morning,
the phone began to ring.
The man I felt was in charge answered it,
pulled out the wire of the receiver, and said,
"That's us. We are away now".
They left all the doors lying wide open and went off in my car.
I closed the front door and I said to the wains,
"That's the car gone. Your daddy will be home soon."

The last time, Patsy was released, the car was blown up.
So I thought that's what was going to happen again.
But it's not what happened.
This time they chained Patsy to a van,
loaded it with one thousand pounds of explosives,
made him drive to the army checkpoint
and then detonated it remotely.

Soon after this, Patsy's brother and wife came up,
and then, the media.
Hordes of them.
I knew there had been a big explosion and
that soldiers had been killed.
And then it came on the news and it showed our car,
parked across the road,
and I thought,
Holy shit!

The worst for me, is that I think that from midnight on,
Patsy knew that he was going to die.
They couldn't let him go, knowing he could be recognised,
and they would have had to take their masks off to cross the border.
I think that Patsy had four hours
knowing that he was going to be murdered,
wondering how they were gonna kill him.
It must have been hell for him.
But what must have been the worst for him
was knowing he would never see his family again.

Letters

"*Dear Mrs. Gillespie,*
We don't know each other
but for some reason I felt compelled to write and
extend my sympathy to you.
As I picked up the Sunday paper,

*I saw the account of your husband's death and also
of the five British soldiers.
I felt both anger and sorrow.
It's beyond understanding how anyone can have so little regard for
human life and to murder six men like that."*
USA

*"Dear Mrs. Gillespie and family,
When I heard what happened to your family yesterday on
Canadian TV,
I felt that I had to write to you.
I wanted you to know that here are millions of us all over the world
who find terrorism as appalling as you do."*
Canada

*"Dear Mrs. Gillespie,
God be with you. Please know that this congregation holds you
closely in our hearts in prayer and sympathy in your great, great
sadness. May you know that the firm hand of God is more powerful
than this horrible evil.
With sorrow,"*
A parish priest - Donegal

Kathleen

*The hardest thing I ever had to do was try to reach my son Patrick
in England before he saw it on TV.
"I want you to come home now, son."
He said, "I got my ticket, mammy, I'm coming home in December".
"No, I need you to come home now, son. Tom will bring you."
"Why?"
"I'll tell you when you come home."
"'I'm not coming until you tell me why."
That was the worst thing I ever had to do –
to tell him over the phone that his daddy was dead.
I can still hear him screaming,*

"I'll kill those bastards!"
I wanted to identify the body at the mortuary,
but they said, "I'm sorry Mrs. Gillespie. The coffin is closed."
There was nothing to identify.
No final proof of his death.

So until the time of the inquest,
a part of me still thought that Patsy was in hiding somewhere
and that eventually he would phone for me and send me tickets
to bring the wains to wherever he was.
Common sense told me he was dead,
but I was living in constant preparations
to move at a minute's notice.

About a month after his death, there was a howling wind
and lashing rain.
The branches of the rose bush in front of my bedroom window
were scratching against the glass.
I couldn't sleep.
I thought it was Patsy trying to get in through the window.
So at 3am I put me coat on, went out,
and cut the rose bush down to the roots.

At the inquest they talked about the numbered body bags.
I realised that none of them knew what was in the coffin.
I had terrible nightmares about him being put together wrong.
I couldn't sleep with the nightmares.
One night I finally propped myself up with me book and thought:
I'm terrified to go to sleep.
And the next thing,
I looked down at the door,
and Patsy was standing at the door.
Now, I wasn't sleeping. I was propped up.
I had me book in me hand.
I had my glasses on.
I looked at the door and Patsy was standing there
with his grey cardigan that he'd been wearing

when he was taken away.
He said, "Look at me girl. I'm ok. Go to sleep now".
And that was that.

I went to a healing service in the church that Sunday evening,
and the priest preached,
"On the last day when we all arise perfect".
And I thought: This is for me.
Final proof that Patsy was ok wherever he was.

There were days when I got up in the morning and thought:
I can't face this day.
Days when I went back to bed
and stayed there until it was time to get Jennifer from school.
People were coming to me all the time with this terrible tragedy.
I wouldn't allow it to monopolise my life.
Eventually Jennifer said she wouldn't go out with me
to a restaurant for Sunday dinner.

The last time we'd been out, an elderly woman came over.
"Aren't you Mrs. Gillespie?"
When I said "Yes", she looked at her companion,
"I told you it was Mrs. Gillespie".
Other people ducked around, not knowing what to say.
The worst was seeing a friend in town notice me
and then fly into the shoe shop.
I felt lost, being ignored.

I was determined not to let them get the best of me.
They'd killed my husband, but they weren't going to win.
Even at my husband's funeral I didn't cry.
'Cos I thought: I'm not going to let them see
what they've done to me and my family.
I'm not going to give them the satisfaction.

*I never go outside the door without my make-up on,
or without my hair fixed.
Because these men who murdered my husband
are still walking the streets.*

*I knew from the beginning that I had to be strong.
I had so much hatred and rage burning inside of me.
It was consuming me.
At the time I would have liked the five men
who murdered my husband
to be tied up in front of me and let me be free
to do what I wanted with them. Then I changed my mind.
I thought it would be more painful if something bad happened
to someone they loved.
Then they would know how it felt.*

*But hatred was actually manifesting in my body as illness,
and I had to make a conscious decision to abandon it
for the sake of my health.
I decided: Well, then, just leave it in God's hands.
I'll just pass it over. He has broader shoulders than I have.
Now I don't care.
Now I just feel that those men will suffer in their own way.
If not in this life, then in the next.*

*My biggest worry after everything was over was that
I had sixteen and eighteen-year-old sons.
I was worried that
they'd join a paramilitary group
to avenge their father's death.
How was I going to keep them out of trouble?
I don't know whether it was my influence,
or maybe just knowing that their father was a man of peace.
It's one of the things I'm most proud of in my life.*

*What actually brought me back to sanity
was that I became involved in a programme at the
Glencree Peace and Reconciliation Centre,
dialoguing with ex-paramilitaries.*

*I remember the first time it was suggested that I
meet with ex-combatants,
I got dreadful flashbacks.
The very thought of confronting an ex-IRA man
or somebody like that –
to even look at them, never mind talk to them, was horrific.
I just panicked.
I actually got up and ran out of the room.*

*But then I began to say to myself,
If I'm one of the people who wants peace, and I am,
then I need to be prepared to meet these people,
mix with them, talk to them,
and hear their stories and what they have to say.
And if I'm not prepared to do this,
how can I expect other people in Northern Ireland to do this work?*

*So I've been meeting with ex-paramilitaries for the past fifteen years.
Some of them have even become friends.
I confront and challenge them to meet up
with the people they injured.
In terms of justice, things are still up in the air.
Five men were arrested for the crime, but they were let go
after a couple of months because of insufficient evidence.
Some even got compensation for wrongful imprisonment.*

*One of the rawest wounds is that Patsy
was described as being 'a legitimate target of war'.
I'd really like that explained to me.
I'm waiting for the HET's final conclusion about suspected collusion.
I have evidence of foreknowledge.*

I had become reconciled to the idea of the IRA being the baddies,
but if it's proven that our government,
who are supposed to be looking after us,
actually masterminded the whole thing…
Well, it doesn't bear thinking about.

Letter

"Dear Mrs. Gillespie,
Thank you for talking with us yesterday in your time of grief.
As an experienced journalist, it was unexpectedly honouring
to witness your sorrow. Hopefully someone, somewhere will have
been so touched by your words that they might turn away from
violence. My deepest sympathy is with you and your family."
A journalist

Kathleen

Twenty years have passed, and I continue my work with ex-
combatants and am still active in pursuing the case for justice.
I won't give up.
My family has grown, and I'm now the grandmother of
four beautiful babies.
My eldest son Patrick wears his father's wedding ring –
the one he left on the kitchen cabinet.
I feel Patsy on my shoulder guiding special people to me,
to help and guide me through.
He is always with me giving me strength.

When I was picking Patsy's headstone,
I wanted to write, "Murdered by the IRA".
But instead, I had them engrave the words:
"Lord, let him be an instrument of thy peace."
I pray he did not die in vain.

Lord, let him be an instrument of thy peace.

Letters from Around the World

Kathleen loves being a grandmother. Over the past thirty-two years, she has prioritised family life, holding her three children and six grandchildren close. Yet, while attending to her family, she has also dedicated herself to ensuring that Patsy did become an instrument of God's peace. Her clarion call for justice, her willingness to work with and befriend ex-combatants in the name of peace, and her relentless offering of her story for the sake of future generations, are just some of the ways she has dedicated her life towards this mission.

The impact of Patsy's death was felt internationally. When I first interviewed Kathleen at her house, she asked me if I wanted to read some of the hundreds of letters that she had received from people worldwide. Twenty years later, she still had them in a box on a shelf in her closet. We spread them about her living room and chose eight to be read in the production. They were from men, women, young and old, who wanted to express their outrage and sympathy. Many of the envelopes arrived with incomplete addresses, such as, "Patsy Gillespie's widow, Derry". But they arrived and brought comfort.
The fact that years before social media, the lengths that ordinary people went to, in order to offer Kathleen condolences, was profound. When I read all the letters at once, I was struck by the universality of grief, and how one horrific murder united so many people around the world.

Perhaps the most surprising ripple effect of the letters happened about a year after the premiere of the *I Once Knew a Girl* production. A documentary film about our project was shown on the BBC. Afterwards, I got a call from the vice-principal of one of the schools in Derry. He was watching the documentary when he recognised one of the letters being read. It was the letter he had written to Kathleen as a seventeen-year-old student. (John p.163/4)

Now twenty-one years later, John Harkin was moved that

his letter had meant so much to Kathleen that she had kept it all these years. He asked if they could meet, and she was delighted. Following their conversation, he invited her to speak to his students at the Oakgrove School, an integrated primary school. Thus began an ongoing relationship between Theatre of Witness performers and the school, which continues to this day.

Recently, when students at Oakgrove found out that Kathleen would be one of the presenters at a Theatre of Witness workshop, they gleefully reacted: "I told you Kathleen would come! We can't wait to tell Mr. Harkin!"

Healing with Ex-combatants

In addition to many people in Northern Ireland, the Republic and around the world, paramilitary prisoners were also deeply affected by Patsy's death. Many ex-combatants admitted that, when they heard of his horrific death, they realised they no longer wanted to be part of any organisation that would commit such acts of atrocity. It became the tragedy that turned many of them around. And it led to some of them later meeting with Kathleen at Glencree Peace and Reconciliation Centre as part of their own healing work. That training and those relationships are what paved the way for Kathleen to be ready to embark on her Theatre of Witness journey.

> *I went in search of something that I felt I needed. And I was invited to go down to a meeting at Glencree with ex-combatants. When I got there and met the people, I felt at home. I also met up with parents of the soldiers who were killed in the explosion with Patsy. They came from England, and we became friends. I felt that I had found what I needed for me.*
>
> *At Glencree, I did a lot of training for facilitation, mediation,*

and listening skills during the course of that nine years. Then funding stopped and I wondered: Where do I go next? But a wonderful opportunity came like a bright light in a tunnel. I met Teya, which led me to a completely different way of working for peace and reconciliation. We went on stage and the work was more visible. It brought it home for people.

Beginning the Theatre of Witness Journey

We invited Kathleen to attend the premiere of *We Carried Your Secrets*, because, in the production, Robin, the former RUC officer, spoke about being on the body recovery team after the Coshquin bomb. We wanted to prepare her that he would be talking about Patsy's death, and we wanted to make sure she was supported.

Kathleen was one of the first people to stand up in the Q & A following the performance. I remember being struck by the power of both her presence and voice. She was visibly moved and thanked us. She then said she had two questions.

The first - she wanted to know whether Robin would meet with her personally, because she had always questioned what actually was in Patsy's coffin. She needed to hear from Robin what he knew from having been at the scene. Luckily, he was honoured to meet with her, which they did in private. Each of them later reported how meaningful their conversation was. That was the beginning of a deep relationship of trust that endures to this day.

Kathleen then asked me if she could be in our next Theatre of Witness production. I had announced that it would be performed by women affected by the Troubles. I was touched that someone of Kathleen's stature volunteered herself in this public space. What I soon discovered, was that while people in Northern Ireland knew about Patsy's murder, they didn't know the story from Kathleen's perspective. She hadn't yet had the opportunity to share what the tragedy and aftermath were like for her and their children beyond her work at Glencree. And she very much wanted to.

I had to stay strong

After Patsy's death, I contemplated suicide. But I realised that my children had nobody but me. I could have turned to drink or become reclusive, but I knew I had to stay strong to raise them. This is what got me involved in Peace and Reconciliation.

I still have 'hide my head' days. But when I am out, I dress as well as I can and wear make-up. The men who murdered Patsy still walk the streets. I wouldn't know who they are because their faces were covered with balaclavas. But early on, I realised that I could one day be walking past one of them and I didn't want them to think they'd brought me down to another level. I have pride.

Kathleen and Anne

That pride and strength is perhaps what made Katheen's first encounter with Anne, a former IRA quartermaster, so powerful. They met in our very first full group meeting, although each had been briefed about the other. When I asked the group who wanted to start off our sharing, Kathleen quickly raised her hand. I knew however, that if she told her story first, Anne may have been too overwhelmed by the guilt and fear for having been part of the IRA to speak. So I suggested instead, that she go first.

Kathleen, like all the women, listened intently. But she listened with a willingness to really hear what had drawn

Anne into becoming a member of the IRA. It was obvious how painful it was for her to hear Anne's story. But Kathleen held strong, and her previous peace work held her in good stead. Afterwards she hugged Anne and said, "It's ok".

I recognised in Kathleen a great capacity for compassion and understanding, and I knew that our group process could take us deep into territory none of us had traversed before. That compassion which Kathleen showed Anne established the foundation for their relationship to blossom into the deep friendship that it's become today. While their stories aren't linked directly, people easily could imagine that Kathleen would harbour hatred towards anyone who had been part of the IRA. But Anne and Kathleen have overcome so many of their initial fears and feelings, and they now bring out the best in each other.

Kathleen's modelling of compassionate listening has also echoed throughout our entire group. It set the stage for all the women to authentically express themselves while simultaneously being open to their differences.

Whenever the production of *I Once Knew a Girl* toured throughout Northern Ireland, Kathleen worried about the potential danger Anne could be in, both from the IRA, and the government. She became protective of her and was always the first to publicly proclaim the courage it took for Anne to share her story onstage.

> **I was frightened every night that we went on stage when Anne said, "I am an ex-member of the IRA ".**
>
> My heart would just go out of my chest. I thought: Who's in the audience that's going to take this on board and approach her? And she was approached many times about many things.
>
> I was stopped on the street one day, and a lady said to me: 'I saw you on TV the other night". This was in the documentary that Anne and I had done together. "It's great what you're doing, but how can you even sit beside that

> woman, never mind talk to her and work with her?"
> I just was so horrified at what she said, that I looked at her and replied, "You know something? It's people with your attitude that's keeping this thing going." And I just turned and walked away.
>
> Other times when people ask how I can work with "That woman Anne", I tell them how much she has helped me now. Then you see the light in their eyes. "If that works for her, maybe it can work for someone else like me, too."

Recently Kathleen had a bad fall and Anne offered to help care for her. She became her driver, and Kathleen now jokingly calls Anne her 'personal assistant'. Anne helps her with all manner of everyday activities, including getting on the internet and social media. They often present workshops together and call each other close friends.

Forgiveness

Because they are so close, people sometimes assume that Kathleen has forgiven Anne for her role in the IRA. They also think she has forgiven the other ex-IRA combatants who have turned their lives around, and possibly even forgiven the men who murdered Patsy. But that isn't true. Kathleen believes that forgiveness isn't hers to give. And although she will work closely with ex-combatants, listening and trying to understand what led then to commit the acts that they did, she is adamant that she will never forgive.

> People take it for granted that because I'm doing this peace work, that I forgive the men who murdered Patsy. I make it very clear that, no, I have no forgiveness for them. They sat around a table and planned his death, which indiscriminately killed five other people. People ask, "Well, what would you do if one of those five men who was in your house that night, came to your door and asked for your forgiveness? What would you do?"

> **If someone who murdered Patsy came to my home
> and asked for my forgiveness,
> I would tell him that he was
> more than welcome to come to my house.**
>
> **I would sit him down, give him a cup of tea or coffee.
> But I am not giving him forgiveness.**
>
> *They're only looking forgiveness for themselves and their own conscience. They're not looking for forgiveness to do me any good.*
>
> *As people get older, their conscience starts to bother them about things that they did when they were younger. That's painful because there's very little that they can do about what they've done. They can't bring my husband back.
> When they ask for my forgiveness, it's for their own conscience, and not for me.*
>
> *I pray for these men every night. I pray that they can't sleep because their conscience is bothering them. I pray that they're suffering in some way.*
>
> *I would be glad for the men who murdered Patsy to feel remorse. That remorse would ease their conscience. And I would say, "I'm glad you know that you've done wrong. You've listened to my story and I'm glad of all that. But I'm not granting you forgiveness to ease your conscience. I'm just telling you that I understand what you're saying, and why you're suffering now. But at the same time, I'm glad you're suffering."*

At the core, nothing shakes Kathleen from her moral stance.

> *I just cannot believe that people can just indiscriminately murder people. Why do they think it's alright to do that?*

Kathleen's firm clarity about forgiveness may seem surprising. I think many people associate forgiveness with peace-making and may even think of them as interdependent. But forgiveness is a deeply personal and spiritual matter independent of peace-making.

I've learned from Kathleen that the pressure to forgive is an imposition on victims that often feels like a violation. It has nothing to do with the victim's ability or willingness to engage in deep and compassionate discussions with those who have caused great harm. Those discussions take tremendous courage, strength and understanding from all parties, and often lead to real and lasting reconciliation. Friendship too, regardless of whether there has ever been forgiveness. Choosing not to forgive has in no way impeded Kathleen's peace work, and certainly not her ongoing friendships with ex-combatants.

Public Storytelling

In the wake of Coshquin, the media constantly approached Kathleen to tell her story and comment on the news. That continues to this day.

> *After Patsy died, I was doing a lot of TV. Someone said, "They're using you". "Yes, I know. But I'm using them. I can speak out." "Aren't you afraid the IRA will do something?" "What more can they do to me?" When the IRA murdered Patsy, a lot of people turned against them. This is my platform to let the world know what happened and to know how I feel.*
>
> **It's a pulpit for me to tell the world how I feel.**

Theatre of Witness has become another kind of pulpit or platform for Kathleen to share her story. One in which she had total control over how her story was edited and presented. And which was built on the healing power of relationships

Theatre of Witness is more fun than talking to the media. We had all of us together. We had good times and bad times, but we always had the togetherness. Before that, it was just me on my own. This was a whole new thing. There was so much support, so many people

looking out for you, and a whole group of new friends who had my back.

This was a different closeness – the closeness of friends.

Amnesty and Memories

At the time of this writing, Northern Ireland is now discussing giving amnesty to all for political crimes before 1998. That means there will be no further investigations or prosecutions related to Patsy's murder, or for any of the other atrocities committed before the Peace Agreement was signed.

They say we should have forgotten by now.

At this moment in time, I, along with thousands of other people who were bereaved before 1998, feel dismissed. I can see in my mind's eye, a whole group of politicians standing up and just turning their backs on me and saying, "Right, you don't matter anymore. You should have forgotten about it by now."

How can you forget something like that? It's ridiculous. They don't intend to do anything now about the victims before 1998. It's all been dismissed.

It makes you feel so small, when they're actually telling me, 'That was then, and you would have forgotten about it by now. You've had plenty of time since 1998 to worry about it and forget about it. And you should be continuing on with your life now." You know it's ridiculous.

Recently the Secretary of State for Northern Ireland was challenged to meet with Kathleen so he could explain his reasoning for supporting amnesty. Kathleen met him at Stormont.

I wanted to know why 1998 was the watershed. One of the ladies from his office sat beside the Secretary of State. And she made a very, very stupid comment, and I picked her apart right away. She talked about "faded memories".

I said: "You use the wrong words, because you have no clue what you're talking about. If you could sit with hours to spare, I could tell you every single minute of those six hours that those men were in my house, without forgetting any detail of it. And that was thirty-one years ago!"

"Don't you talk to me about faded memories."

I wasn't letting her off with it. Letting somebody off with a statement like that? She doesn't know what she's talking about. I challenged them.

I said, "I would like you to step into my shoes for a day and try and make yourself think about what happened to my husband. How those people sat down and planned it all and how they did what they did. And see how you would feel if it was your home and they took your partner away!"

"You put yourself in my place after fighting a case of collusion for all these years, and now find out that there will be no more investigations. How would you feel?"

This decision that there will be no more prosecutions, means that, as Robin has stated: **"All we have left is our stories"**.

Storytelling

*There's a difference between 'storytelling'
and sharing your life story.
It's your life.
It's not storytelling,*

As time passes, the importance of sharing Theatre of Witness stories in Northern Ireland has increased. Imparting the lived experiences of people who were affected by the Troubles has become a significant method for ensuring that the factual truth of what happened in a time of war gets preserved. But the stories in Theatre of Witness also ensure that the emotional truth gets passed on to younger generations, many of whom still carry sectarian hatred without having examined the sources and the legacy.

> *These are important stories. People can learn from what happened before. It's documented. If we document it, people will learn the real story.*
>
> *At my grandson's school there was a substitute teacher in history class who told the story about my husband's death. He had the wrong details. My grandson said, "That's my grandfather you're talking about". At first, the teacher didn't believe him. He was very nonchalant. Jude gave him evidence and details to prove that he really was Patsy's grandson. That man wasn't teaching the facts. Rather, he was teaching the facts as he saw them. And even after Jude told him the truth, he kept on with his story.*
>
> *If someone is going to teach about Patsy's murder, they need to know the truth. It needs to be documented from the people it happened to. Otherwise, in one hundred years' time, it could be told differently.*

Violence and bomb scares continue to take place in Northern Ireland. In a sense, they too are the ripple effects. Recently, Kathleen and her daughter went to the centre of Derry, parked their car, and made their way to the Richmond Centre to shop. But everything was cordoned off and the mall was evacuated. A suspected device was found.

> *I just felt sick. And I'm sure I wasn't the only one. There were hundreds of people there. And I'm sure plenty of them had lost people in the Troubles, and the thought of a bomb scare... It's been so long since we had anything like that. It used to be that you couldn't get into town without coming across a bomb scare.*
>
> *The very thought that it could start up again, left me so ill*

and so distressed. It was like re-traumatising of all the bomb scares before everything stopped.

It made me think about our next generation. Are our grandchildren going to be caught up in something like this? It's just sickening, it really is. It's stressful even to think about it.

Ongoing Workshops

I feel very proud of what I've done since Patsy's death.

I feel that I have let the whole world know exactly how I feel. And I just feel so proud of Patsy. It's been proven that Patsy saved many soldiers on the army base. At the minute before his death, he called out that there was a bomb. How could you not feel proud of that? There are a lot of people who have been murdered in this conflict. And they don't get all the privileges and opportunities that I've had.

There's no way I'm condoning Patsy's death. But I am proud to know that I haven't sat down and done nothing. I have used Patsy's death to forward the work that I'm doing within peace and reconciliation.

Most of the ongoing Theatre of Witness work in Northern Ireland is now in the form of peacebuilding workshops. Kathleen is one of the more ardent facilitators. She speaks of being energised by being with participants; especially students as young as twelve years old.

Some of the questions the children ask are unbelievable. They are so inquisitive. They want to know what happened and why. And they want to know why the people who murdered Patsy aren't in prison and paying for what they did.

I get a buzz from meeting new people and their questions. I come home mentally and physically exhausted, but it's so exhilarating. It's the act of passing on information that people don't know but want to know. It's a great feeling.

Non-violence and peace-making are dreams that we all have. It's a real dream, to think that for our next generation, it's going to be peaceful. And there's not going to be any more of this killing and all this stuff that's going on. That's what we're working towards.

I'll never get tired of doing this work until I can't walk out of the front door.

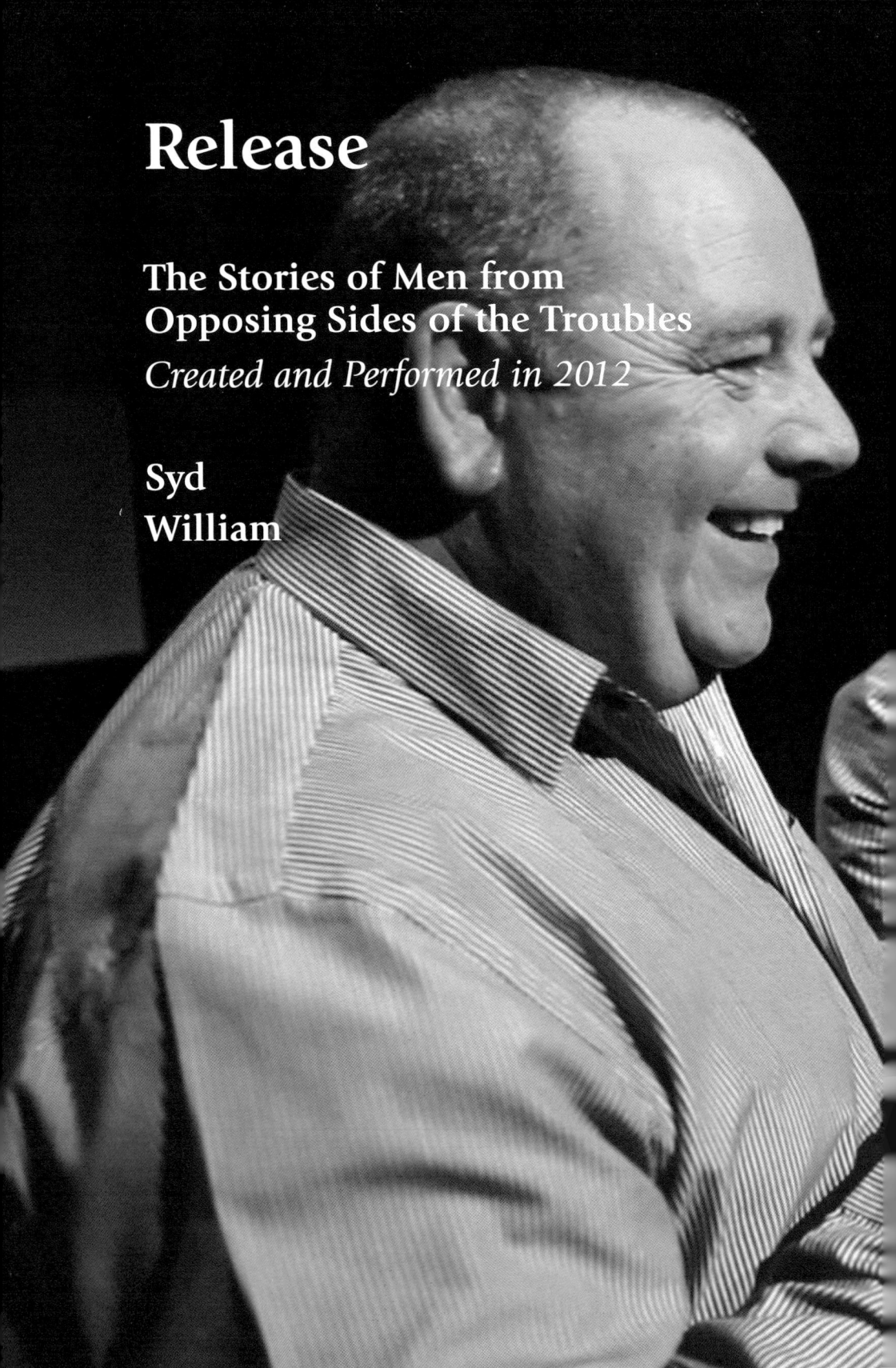

Release

The Stories of Men from Opposing Sides of the Troubles
Created and Performed in 2012

Syd
William

The Eyes that See All

Syd Trotter

There's a line in the sand.
The man I was before, and the man I'm becoming.

Which history will judge me?

Sometimes I walk the fields with my metal detector.
I like history. I like to find things - the excitement of the search.
Every inch you go down into the ground is one hundred years.
My detector goes down fifteen to nineteen inches,
and it's only 1900 years ago.
We just scrape the surface of history.

Once I found a massive horseshoe.
Looking back, you can imagine people in the field playing,
the horse throwing the shoe.
I find a lot of Coke tops,
but I've also found part of an army belt buckle,
musket balls and a thruppence.

I picture soldiers firing musket balls in battles of anger.
Each object has a story, a history.
People ask me,
"Why do you metal detect in those fields where there was a famine?
There's nothing of value there."
But history isn't made up only of things of value.
That's why I go into those fields.
It's the thrill of wondering what I might find and
imagining who came before us.

I've always been interested in finding things.
When I was eleven, I found a homemade rocket launcher.
Two weeks later my brother found a Russian RPG.
We knew enough to know there was something wrong.
We told my father who'd been in the police.
He closed the road, called the army
and they did a controlled explosion.
Later I found nine warheads and mortars in a small dirty lane.
It didn't make our family popular.
The community saw it as me giving their things away.

I became a bit of a target and was bullied.
It had an impact on school, and I became quite angry.
I remember my mother saying to my father,
"Billy, we have to get out of here".
But he was stubborn and wouldn't be chased by anyone.

I grew up in a house and time where the abnormal became normal.
But what is normal, unless you have something else
to compare it with?
One of our houses was a farmhouse. I'll never forget it.
There was no electricity, a tin bath, and more mice than children.
It was a dreadful place, but it was home.
My father was in the police,
and we were aware of the potential dangers.

We knew not to open the door at night
unless my father was standing around the corner,
armed and ready.
I had a friend who lived four houses up whose father
was blown up as a policeman.
That was the first funeral I went to.
I seen his wife. She was crying. "Please Ronnie, don't leave… no!"
Once you see that…
I was twelve.

I never felt like I belonged anywhere or to anyone.
We planted ourselves here, but we came from nothing ourselves.
The weeds of the earth.
We're still weeds here.
Historically we didn't get taught Irish history. We were taught the
War of the Roses.
It's not my identity,
but it has a load of unanswered questions for me.
I never felt a brotherhood.
I would always be a bit of a loner.
Even when I got involved.
I got involved out of anger.
Someone close to me was arrested for murder.
He'd been exploited.
My anger was at those who gave him the means to do it.
I had hatred towards them.
I got involved first by collecting money for prisoner welfare.
Then it got took a sinister turn.

If I came to you and said, "I'm looking for money for prisoners",
it would have been hard for you to say "No".
I never needed to say anything else.
I just that I said I was collecting money for prisoners.
Your mind would have done the rest.
That was racketeering.

Builders who came into our areas had to pay.
It was an implied threat.
I didn't think of the pain or hurt I caused to anyone then.
I was a menace.
There's no nice way of demanding money.
It was like being swallowed up in a cyclone;
something you get caught up in.
It was a relief to finally be captured.
It ended it.
Though at the time I didn't think it.
But if I hadn't been caught, I could be dead now.
I remember the detective saying,
"I don't want you back in my area anymore.
I don't want another dead body on my hands."

I got thirty-four years – three tens and a four.
I did five and a half years.
I was sent to Magilligan for a few years. Had to slop out.
Then they moved me to the Maze;
not the loyalist wing, but to the kitchen.
I fought to get moved.
My daughters were just two and three at the time.
They were eight and nine when by the time I got out.

It hardened me.
There's a black side to my character.
I can remember being on remand in 1988,
and going to church to meet others from other wings.
A minister said, "
Don't let the light go out of your eyes".
I still remember it to this day.
My interpretation was: if you take someone's life,
the light goes out of your eyes.
They get a lost dead look about them.
I often thought of that.
If you were to take someone else's life,

you'd kill the light within yourself.
You lose your own soul.
I've met people who killed people while in jail
and there is a deadness in their eyes.
I would never have wanted to lose my soul.

I wouldn't be glorifying anything the paramilitaries done.
Anything they done; it's about hurt and pain to someone.
Doesn't matter who it is.
Loyalist or nationalist or those fighting for Mother Ireland.
In the end it's all about pain. Chipping away at someone else.
I can't see the sense in it anymore. No logic in it.
The only space I can own is the space where I now stand.

I am drawing a line in the sand
Who I was before and who I am now.

I am a husband, father, grandfather.
I am a community worker.
I see things differently now.
Now it's up to people like me to rebuild what's broken.

We are the guardians of our own souls.
We are the vessels of our own hate.
We are the witnesses who said nothing.
We are the eyes that see all.

Eyes

When I first met Syd, I saw how deeply he looked at the world, his time and place in history, and the roles he and others have played in the conflict. He's a man who has watched and pondered since he was a young child; understanding how abnormal it was to grow up in extreme poverty, and in a place where he felt he never belonged - a sectarian war zone. Wisdom has grown from his reflections.

One of the most poignant parts of Syd's story for me was the advice the prison minister gave him. *"Don't let the light go out of your eyes."* This was the only time Syd talked about the effects of a positive influence on him. A moment which he never forgot.

> *I firmly believe the eyes are mirror of the soul. You can see deadness in some people's eyes as if they've lost their way. And in many ways, it's sorrow as well. But they can't admit to that sorrow. Because to do so, would open up a can of worms for them. And that might be something that they cannot get back into the can.*
>
> *My eyes aren't dead because I never killed anyone. It was something that I just wasn't prepared to do. The cause or the conflict didn't mean that much to me that I would take somebody's life. I just couldn't. I always thought there was maybe another route that could have been taken.*

Influencers

That other route is where Syd has focused his attention. He has reflected deeply on the various causes that have kept the continuation of the conflict alive. And he has dedicated himself to finding alternative paths other than violence.

> *Now I ask the question: Who influenced me and why did I let myself get influenced?*
>
> *Now I recognise that we don't work in isolation. Everything we believe has been learned. From a young age, I recognised I was a Protestant and took on the views of my father.*
>
> *If I was born in the States, I wouldn't have been a loyalist paramilitary. It wouldn't have entered my head. That said,*

> *depending on where an individual lives, whether it is Harlem or one of the ghettos, those places influence a person. That's not an excuse for what an individual does. But it does give shape to the direction that they have taken in their life.*
>
> *There was a team involved in all of it, and who were they? What were their roles? What did they do? Probably the best way I can talk about it is with the idea of teamwork. We each had a role to play. Someone was just the penalty taker for us in the football match. We played the ball up to them, they took the penalty, they scored the goal.*
>
> *I would never try and justify what I've done because I acknowledge that was wrong. But back then there would have been a whole lot of people who would have been shouting at the TV and maybe would have agreed with what I did at the time.*

When Syd was a young boy, he was surrounded by all the systemic signifiers of sectarianism and violence. His father's colleague in the police was blown up by a bomb. The conflict was raging around him, and he got involved in paramilitary activity. Syd's brother served fourteen years for murder and Syd served six for racketeering. Maturity and hindsight have reshaped his views and life choices.

> *Every day when I when was involved (in the paramilitary organisation), I didn't think of the dangers. I had no fears because the adrenaline was always running. It's only been afterwards when I got older and I started thinking and talking to other combatants, who I meet every day, that I understand more.*
>
> *One friend of mine says that now he's just glad that he wakes up every morning and realises that he's breathing. Because back in the day, we didn't think about that We didn't know whether our doors were gonna get kicked in. We didn't know whether we were going to wake up or not.*

If I was to meet myself now as I was then,
I wouldn't be my friend.
I wouldn't like that person

Taking Accountability

One of the more striking things about Syd is his ability to see his and other young people's lives in context of history. Yet he doesn't absolve himself of his own role in the conflict.

> **We have to acknowledge our own role and how we became who we became.**
>
> *As I get older, I think about my past, not just the things I was involved in, but all the circumstances that got someone like me into prison. When I was a young boy, I hadn't the life experiences to understand what was happening. Back then everything was 'in the moment'. We hadn't time to think. Every day was different. With someone young, who has nothing to measure, how do they react to such a conflict? And when other people die around them, it has an impact.*
>
> *Now through self-reflection, I can see what went on and why. I also see the impact of my actions. But that's all hindsight.*

Post-Prison

Since Syd was released from prison, he has worked towards peace and reconciliation at the community level by working at interfaces between Protestant and Catholic communities. He uses theatre and dialogue, often between communities, and sometimes negotiates between paramilitaries and community members.

> *In the mid-nineties and up to the early 2000s, I did community-building work at interfaces. Most of the people I*

> dealt with were younger people. I didn't want them to look up to how I had been in the day.

> **There doesn't have to be a winner and a loser**

> I understood both communities. I was trying to get people to give way. But people thought that if they gave away something, they were giving in and losing. But actually, it makes you the bigger person. There doesn't have to be a winner and a loser. I tried to make people understand that it's good to give way. You get more out of it for you and your community.

Becoming Part of Theatre of Witness

When the opportunity arose to be part of the cast of *Release*, Syd, a strong believer in the power of theatre to effect change, was open to joining.

> I decided to join Theatre of Witness because I like to challenge myself, and I knew from the outset that it would be a challenge. It allowed me to speak for myself about how I felt, and why I was who I was. That was a massive thing.

> It also allowed me to see the consequences of the conflict on someone like William, a former prison governor. I was able to almost get into his head and understand what he went through. That was the best thing for me.

> It was also personal. It was about finding out more about myself. And I suppose, in many ways, it's validation for what someone's done, or why they've done it

The Unlocking

Theatre of Witness was the opening of the door.

Theatre of Witness brought everything back to me, including the hurt, pain, and anger. But it also gave me the opportunity to reflect on it all.

The hardest part of doing it was when you've locked memories and emotions up for so long and they spill out. You have a job trying to contain them. It's like dropping a bag of marbles when you're a kid. Sometimes doing your best to get them all back in isn't enough. Some of the time, I was angry, probably mostly at myself. As I've gotten older, I realise what I lost. Some things get lost, and you never get them back. You just have to suck it up. 'Release' was just the start. In many ways, it formatted a process that would help each of us as individuals to address some of the issues that we had, and maybe still do have. It was the opening of the door.

There was a peace about it as well.

Emotional Outcomes

For me, this wasn't about theatre. It was very real.

In Northern Ireland people park all their emotions and memories and then leave them. And the problem is; when the car park becomes full, what happens? I think my car park was filled when I started this process. And trying to unpark some of this stuff was difficult. Certainly for me, and maybe for some of the other guys. It opened the door for reflection.

But opening the doors inside of myself that had been locked up, helped me understand other people better. Especially in the course of my work.

I can empathise more with people.

> *There are two types of listening, listening for what you want to hear, and listening to hear everything.*

Syd was one of the steadiest of the men in our group. He was genuinely interested in hearing the stories of everyone. He listened with great attention and non-judgement, framing their stories in the context of history. He also developed a deep friendship with William – the former prison governor of the Maze prison when Syd was a prisoner there. They were the most unlikely of pairs to develop a friendship, but Syd's openness and compassion right from the start guided the beginnings of what has become a treasured friendship for both of them.

> *I can hear everything now. Rather than talk, now I listen more. I'm not angry anymore.*
> *I just park it and think about it.*
>
> *I need to be learning things all the time, but there has to be a project at the end. Theatre of Witness gave me that.*

Progressing Onwards From Theatre of Witness

Syd has continued to work in the peace sector. And his mission has also included going back into education to study for a law degree, at age sixty-one. He's built on his experiences with Theatre of Witness, creating a new workshop design for youth that focuses on the influences in someone's life.

One very effective activity he has devised is to have a participant become a human puppet attached by strings to others acting as influencers.

For Syd, having the world accept part of the responsibility for a person's involvement is the missing piece.

> *I think the one piece that was missing for me in Theatre of*

Witness was the question of turning the lens to look at the influencers. It was enough for a performer to admit that they were guilty and bare their soul to the world. But the other part of the equation is the question of what influenced and moulded the person?

For me, the world must accept part of the responsibility

It's not enough just to blame the person. If a child is starving and becomes a bank robber, the question is: Why did he become that? What influenced him to do that? Now people say: "But not everybody who's starving becomes a bank robber". Thank goodness. But some people will. And why do they?

I'm interested in what comes after Theatre of Witness. After you've told your story, there needs to be an interrogation of the influences. How? Who? Why? What? There's more to our stories. We don't live in isolation.

Syd now intervenes between community members and people in paramilitary groups. People know he has been on both sides, and he has the credibility and experience to facilitate discussions and solutions.

If somebody's afraid or is having issues with the paramilitaries, you can approach them together and ask, "What's the craic? This guy just wants to work, he wants to live. He's a decent guy, you know." It's about confronting your fears. I just think, be yourself and give with integrity, whatever it is. But don't be soft. If something is wrong, say it's wrong. Because people see through that. If you're trying to be all things to all men, it doesn't work.

I've seen the very best and very worst of men and women.

Being a Peacemaker

Change is possible. But politicians haven't changed things. It's the ordinary people who talk across the fence. They recognise their peers. All those smaller things can make something greater happen. There's no leadership that can bring about proper peace. It can be soul-destroying if I think about it, but I just get on with what I do.

For me, it's about becoming a quiet peacemaker. The peacemaker who doesn't run to the news. Who helps the small people, and helps them with the small issues of their lives. It's not the headline grabbers. It's not about that for me. It's all those small things that make a change in somebody's life.

For me, it's about becoming a quiet peacemaker.

The Man Who Tried to Keep Peace

William McKee

The Man who Tried to Keep Peace

A child doesn't grow up dreaming
of one day becoming a prison governor.
It was a quirk of fate that led me down that particular path.
I am a Protestant, born on the 12th of July, 1955,
and my name is William McKee.
However, for the majority of my adult life,
I was always known as Billy.
We lived in the countryside with a tin bath in front of the fire.
We had no electricity and no TV. We were a very poor family.
I remember very little about my life before the age of twelve,
when my mother died of breast cancer.
She was operated on the Monday and died on Wednesday.
I can still see my eight-year-old brother and I
hugging and crying together in the garden.

All my memories of before then are blotted out.
After her death, I couldn't stand other kids approaching me saying,
"I heard your mother died".
So, I arranged to change schools so no one would continually
remind me of my loss.
It was a mistake,
because the new school wasn't as good
from an educational perspective as my old one.
I left after 0 levels and got low-paying jobs,
working firstly on a farm,
but then moving on to the wages department in the
Harland and Wolff shipyard, and finally to a factory in
Downpatrick as a sub-accountant,
where the craic with the women was great,
but the wages were a paltry £30 a week.

One evening I was reading the jobs section of the Belfast Telegraph
and saw an invitation to join the Prison Service for £80 a week.
I had no intention of changing jobs,
where I would have to wear a uniform and guard terrorists,
but I thought if I told my employers about my interest,
they would raise my wages.
They called my bluff,
and I was to spend the next twenty-seven years
working in the Prison Service,
eventually rising to the rank of a Governor in the infamous
Maze Prison, also known as Long Kesh.

I loved my job.
I had a good reputation with the prisoners.
I tried to treat everyone fairly.
I was able to walk down no-go wings,
where no other governor or staff could or would go.
The prisoners would banter, "Get the governor a cup of tea".
Or, "One day you'll get your head taken off",
and I'd say, "Oh Kelly, go get the kettle on".

I felt I had earned their begrudging respect.
During my time employed in the prison,
I was able to fix two of the most important issues for prisoners:
visits and food.
It gave me great confidence and I loved my work.
But it didn't protect me from my share of death threats,
forced home moves, and finally, a total breakdown!

One particular day I was on duty at the Maze
and was called to the visiting block
where one of the paramilitary leaders
was sitting angrily with his cohorts.
They were furious about the state of their visiting room.
Their leader was going ballistic. All the staff were in riot gear.
I went in to try to calm things down.

The leader screamed at me:
"Would you let your children come to this visiting room?"
I told him, "I wouldn't bring my children anywhere near this jail"

He introduced me to the prisoners and their visitors by saying:
"This is Governor McKee, who says
he wouldn't bring his kids anywhere near this jail,
but he expects you to bring your children here!"
All of a sudden, I was surrounded by eighty men.
Staff pulled the alarm; the doors were sealed!
I saw rage - all directed at me.
Sweat was pouring down my face.
I was shaking. I probably went white.
I think I just stood there. Their leader just stood there.
Then a grille opened. I made my escape.
I heard the grille lock behind me.

The next day they wrecked their H-Block.
They wanted me killed.

They knew where I lived.
Soon the police were at my house
talking to me about drive-by shootings.
They had evidence to support the death threats.
Our house was close to the road,
and my three children slept upstairs under dormer windows.
I remember looking at my wife.
"We have to move."
She was devastated.
I was overcome by worry and fear for the lives of my three children.
We were gone within three days.
This was just the first of three such forced moves.

The danger never stopped me.
I just kept working, earning more money than we needed,
and putting my priorities in all the wrong places
But I loved my job.

One night at the Maze, an escape tunnel was found.
We had to do full cell searches.
I was in charge of H4 Block,
where one hundred prisoners
were on the doors protesting.
My staff was looking at me for leadership.

None of them would go down the wings.
I went in - alone,
not even a radio.

After it was over, I went into my office where I collapsed.
I was like a puppet with its strings cut.
Another death threat.
The IRA leader had looked me right in the eye:
"You were told yesterday that you were a dead man walking.
When it happens to you, you will know why!'"
There was worse to come.

*A high-profile prisoner was murdered at the Maze, on a day
when I was the governor in charge of the prison.
His organisation, the LVF, blamed me.
There was a whole cascade of events that pointed to collusion,
and the Prison Service never did anything to convince anyone
that I had nothing to do with it.*

*Word was put out to get me.
They had my name and address and knew which car I drove.
When I told my wife that we had to move again, she said,
"I'm not going to let them drive me out of my home a second time!"
How could I blame her?
She had to be carried out of the house, screaming and crying.*

*Eventually the stress was too much, and
one day she told me not to come home anymore.
She was frightened that our children might be seriously harmed.*

*In 2003, the cork just popped on my bottle.
I came into work one day, shaking and white,
and ended up leaving in the back of an ambulance.
The doctor thought it was a heart attack,
but it was PTSD brought on by all the anxiety and stress.*

I went on medical leave and began therapy.

*Within a three-week span, I'd lost my family,
home, work, and health.
My psychiatrist diagnosed me as being suicidal.
He ordered my personal protection weapon to be taken off me.
It took the Prison Service three days to come and collect it and
I became more paranoid,
suspecting everyone of collusion and wanting me dead.
My doctor thought it best if I did not live alone,
so I moved in with my brother.
But within six weeks,*

I was told that a paramilitary group were looking for a big hit,
had identified me and they were on their way.
Police gave me an hour to get out.
I had to call my brother and tell him not to come home.
I felt I was hurting everyone I touched.
It pushed me over the edge.

I went on tablets and began to wish only to be asleep.
When I was awake, I'd count the hours
until I could take more sleeping tablets,
and pray to God that I'd fall asleep quickly.
This was my only escape.
I had sixty-five sessions of counselling.
Mostly I just cried.
My therapist was a wonderful man who said to me,
'William, we'll get through this together".
And eventually, we did.

I am the eternal optimist

Meeting William

While recruiting men to collaborate on *Release*, I never thought I'd be lucky enough to entice William, a former governor in the Maze prison, to join our group. His was a voice that hadn't been heard much in dialogues about peace. What's more, and in his position, he had experienced the very centre of the struggle. I never would have known about him or his story, had I not been meeting with his brother-in-law, who suggested that William might be a good candidate for Release. After our first conversation, I was hooked.

> *Teya's enthusiasm for the project sucked me in, making*
> *me want to be involved in it. I felt it was something that*
> *I needed to do within myself, and I felt it would be a very*
> *cathartic experience. I also thought it was a way I could help*

other people who've been through probably much worse than what I went through.

This was further strengthened when I met the other participants. When I spoke to Syd and Kevin (two other performers from Protestant backgrounds,) we felt that this was something that we owed to other victims. To let them hear our story, and to know that no matter how bad things are, you can come out the other side and go on to have a really happy fulfilled life.

Role as Prison Governor

Upon meeting William, I instantly knew that he had not been a typical prison governor. He saw his role, not as punishment enforcement, but rehabilitation. And even when he himself was targeted, he remained even-handed.

In the Maze prison, it was paramount that I had a good working relationship with the prisoners. The prisoners had such an influence on the political situation here, that the mandate I got from Prison Service headquarters was: "Whatever you do, keep a lid on the Maze". Otherwise, things spilled onto the street and people died. So, my role was always about building working relationships with the prisoners.

When people received a prison sentence, they weren't put in the prison for me to inflict punishment on them. My role was to rehabilitate them, so that when they were released, they would steer away from crime. But with the paramilitaries, it was different, because these were people who were dedicated to a cause.

The paramilitary prisoners were people who had murdered friends and colleagues of mine. But somehow, I was able to rise above it and just do my job.

I was the man who had to be carried away.

I quickly grasped, that, in addition to sharing historically important stories related to his role as a prison governor during the Troubles, William was also willing to be emotionally open and honest about what being in that job had cost him.

> *I served four tours of duty in the Maze prison. I worked through the Dirty Protest and the Hunger Strike, and I was actually on duty the day that thirty-eight republican prisoners escaped through the front gate of the prison.*
>
> *I lost my family, my home, my career, my health, and I almost lost my life through threats of murder and thoughts of suicide.*

William's Book

William never would have been ready to engage with Theatre of Witness had he not first begun his healing process with therapy and the writing of his memoir, *Governor: Inside the Maze*. (Amazon.co.uk). The desire to write grew from his therapy sessions for the PTSD he suffered as a result of his work

> *It took sixty-six sessions of counselling just to get me back to a point where I could actually manage my illness. Part of my therapy was to jot down my jumbled thoughts and memories that we would later dissect and organise at my next therapy session. Those jottings actually became the foundation for my book.*
>
> *The second reason for writing my book, was that the majority of stories told about the conflict are from a republican, prisoner or nationalist perspective. It's very important that the stories of others are also listened to, heard, and understood.*
>
> **No stories are more important than others.**

To write the book, William signed up for a six-week pharmaceutical clinical trial, where he was locked in a room for twenty-three hours a day with his food and accommodation provided. It aided him in finding the discipline to write without distraction. But being locked in did something more. He got to feel what it was like to walk in prisoners' shoes.

> *Whenever I was a governor in the prison, I thought I understood how people must have felt being locked up in a cell at night. But when I did that drug trial, it showed me that, when people have their freedom removed, it is almost the ultimate sacrifice. Apart from your life, the next worst thing is to have your freedom removed.*
>
> *I turned myself into a prisoner to give myself the freedom that I needed to write my book.*

The Theatre of Witness Collaboration

Serving as a prison governor and writing a book had both been somewhat lonely activities. Theatre of Witness was a natural next step. The ongoing collaboration of creating, performing and touring *Release*, enabled William to develop lasting relationships, while continuing to heal the trauma he had experienced. Additionally, and maybe more importantly, he received immediate feedback from the other five participants, as well as thousands of audience members. Their enthusiasm and tears proved that William's story had reached them. His story mattered.

It all started with our initial listening sessions. Our group included former loyalist and republican prisoners, a retired police officer, a former British soldier who had served in both Afghanistan and NI, and a Catholic man who had survived a car bomb as a child.

> *Theatre of Witness was about creating a neutral space where I had a place to engage and listen properly.*
>
> *It taught me to listen better with an open mind to other people's stories. Especially people on the other side, republican and loyalist. I had been an enemy to them all. All the organisations had wanted to murder me.*
>
> *It wasn't like I would go to sit in a cafe and have engagement with a UDA or IRA member. Teya's facilitation created a neutral space.*

William is someone with great people skills, who had been able to disarm many prisoners and staff with what he calls his 'likeability' factor. This stood him in great stead as a member of our group among men from various sides of the conflict.

Confessions

After our very first group meeting, Syd, a former loyalist prisoner who had been incarcerated at the Maze at the time William had been governor, walked out of the theatre with him. Syd volunteered that he believed William had been shafted by the prison administration. They had allowed William to take all the blame for suspected collusion in the murder of loyalist leader Billy Wright. It took an act of courage for Syd to side with William, even all these years later.

> *Syd stuck up for me, and he was understanding from day one. From then on, he and I became great friends.*

Later, William took part in a large workshop in Craigavon filled with many people who had been deeply involved in the conflict. We sat in a big circle that filled the room, and William shared his story.

As always, when he talked about the death threats on him

and his family, William's voice shook and tears came to his eyes. A man in the audience also began crying. Through tears and sobs, he admitted he had been part of that very paramilitary group that had planned the threats to William's life. Witnessing up close the pain and trauma William had endured, the man broke down and apologised. Silence filled the room and William became speechless. Luckily, the facilitators were wonderful in supporting the man. We all breathed together and eventually were able to move the workshop forward as a whole. And following the workshop, the man received further help.

This was a powerful moment that shone light on the interconnectedness of people's stories. We never know the traumas that people in the audience have experienced. We never know what their level of involvement in the violence of the Troubles may have been. Or whether what they choose to share in a workshop is even the truth.

But we do know that bearing witness to a performer's story can be the catalyst that unlocks powerful memories and emotions in an audience member. The role model presented by a performer's truth telling, openness and vulnerability often gives courage to those who witness it. With the right support, that can begin the next step on a journey of healing. William's vulnerability that day provided the spark. Not only for the man who confessed his involvement, but for many who were present for the entire exchange.

'Release' was cathartic.

Former Enemies Create Community

With Theatre of Witness, there was no walking away from any of the pain.

We heard each other's stories over and over again. We became a close group, dependent on each other. It was our role to project to the audience that we were people who were once enemies, now working together. Maybe audience members could look at us and think: "Maybe I can do it, too".

I could not have imagined the feeling it would give me when we first performed, even though I knew we'd deliver. The applause! Here were we, all survivors, now comrades. Mingling with the audience afterwards, people would ask, "How are you still standing? My God, you're fighting to save the rest of us instead of wallowing in self-pity."

My children thought it was amazing. They were very proud and emotional. They hadn't read my book, so the performance gave them a better understanding of what I had gone through.

Not just what I went through, but the rest of the group also. Kevin, the ex-police officer, witnessing 177 murder investigations, and Adrian, a former British soldier, coming to Northern Ireland just before the Omagh bomb.

Our stories are part of the building blocks of peace.

Building Blocks

Both before and after his involvement in Theatre of Witness, William became increasingly sought after as someone who could address issues of peace building in a fair yet deeply personal way.

He was asked to serve on the initial pilot Victim and Survivor

Commission. Due to his ability to create relationships with those on all sides, he got to know Michael McKinley, whose brother was killed on Bloody Sunday.

And recently, one of the members of the Victims Forum, Michael Culbert, invited William to be the surprise guest speaker at the IRA annual conference in County Leitrim. Facing a wall of initial hostility, he put his speech aside and spoke from his heart for an hour and a half.

> *"You will all remember the ten hunger strikers who lost their lives during that tragic period of the conflict. And no doubt you can tell me their names, and the order they died. But can you tell to me just one of the sixteen prison officers murdered during your campaign? Or one of the sixty-five people who died as a result of rioting caused by the Hunger Strike?*
>
> *I know that you have wives, and I know you have children, and I do understand what you've been through. But I need you to listen to my story and understand what I went through. I also had a wife and children, and because of you and your colleagues, I lost my wife and children because of the death threats put upon me."*

William got a standing ovation. He later received a letter from Culbert, who before joining the Victims Forum, had been an IRA prisoner. In his letter, Michael expressed how brave it was for William to come into a room of IRA participants and speak so forthrightly. William now considers his former enemy a colleague.

> *I feel that Micky and I are now going in the same direction. We both want peace in this country.*

The night of the conference, after everyone had gone home, William describes sitting around a table at three o'clock in the morning with six people having a drink.

> *This is what it should be. Six people from the island of Ireland, who want to drink or have a yarn. No orange, no*

> *green, no Protestant, no Catholic. Just six people from the island of Ireland. No suspicions.*

William currently works as an Appropriate Adult, helping people who have been arrested in the streets.

> *I look after them in the system, no matter what crime they've committed, ensuring that they understand everything that's going to happen to them before it happens. Sometimes I get called at 10pm to go help, and I stay up most of the night. If I don't, a young person could be held in a cell overnight, frightened and divorced from his family and loved ones.*

> **Peacebuilding is letting the past go. Learning from it, but not letting it interfere with new growth. It's an ability to get people to listen and accept what we're saying as the way forward.**

Peacebuilding Workshops

Following the performances and film showings of *Release*, William continues to offer workshops through the The Playhouse with Theatre of Witness cast members from three of the productions. The performers show their stories on film and talk about their lives.

> *People hear our horrific stories, and we challenge them. "Is this the way you want to live? Or, you can let us show you another way. We can't go back to having five hundred people being murdered a year."*

> *For those of us who have facilitated workshops through the Playhouse Theatre of Witness Programme, we know the importance of our words to our listeners. When people hear our stories of hurt, anger and forgiveness, we recognise this as the beginning in forming the building blocks of the peace process. This is what helps society to tread the path of peace, as opposed to being drawn back into the dark days of the*

> *conflict.*
>
> *I love doing the workshops, especially the three-day modules in schools. I look at what we do in steering people away from paramilitarism and providing them with a genuine understanding of the past. Because these are kids who grew up after the worst of the Troubles.*
>
> *When Anne (a former IRA member) first heard my story during a performance, the hairs on the back of her neck stood up. She was focused on my job title of Prison Governor, not the person. Now we're close and we work well together delivering workshops. I love her to bits. We tell our stories from the other sides of the wall.*
>
> *The labels that the Theatre of Witness performers once had when we first met – 'former IRA member' or 'former loyalist paramilitary prisoner,' have all gone. We're now just people who live in Northern Ireland.*

One of William's favourite stories concerns a recent workshop with co-performers Kevin and Syd. So there they stood. Kevin, a retired police detective who lost countless officer friends to the Troubles. Syd, a former Loyalist prisoner. And William, an ex-prison governor.

They introduced themselves by name only, then asked the participants to guess who had been a prisoner, or a governor, and who is now a university lecturer. The group assumed that anyone with the name Billy McKee must be a loyalist prisoner and that Kevin Kelly had been in the IRA. They never expected Syd to be a university lecturer.

This exercise provides a valuable lead-in to teaching about assumptions and prejudice, and how people judge each other by names and where they live. William is also delighted that no one expects the three of them to get along so well. The audience can clearly see that they are now good friends.

> *'Release' is one of the best things I've done in my life. I've blossomed and I continue to, years later, facilitating*

workshops and going into rooms with a mixed audience. It's not about the conflict, but about positive steps forward.

When I think about the seeds of Theatre of Witness, I feel that I am a seed myself. I blossom and continue to, eight years later, as I deliver and facilitate workshops for mixed audiences.

It's not about the conflict, but about positive steps forward. Our stories have been part of the building bricks of a shared conflict free-future, and it is so important to keep telling them.

A peacebuilder is someone building peace by talking about the past in such a way that it discourages communities from looking back, and instead, makes them focus on a positive shared future, pulling communities together.

This is about letting the past go, learning from it and not letting it interfere with new growth.

The past becomes the base. We refer to it, but we're moving out, up and away from it.

Future Generations

Without Theatre of Witness, I would not be doing what I'm doing now.

I could not be happier than when I'm standing at the front with the kids and telling them my story and explaining all the reasons why they should never dream of becoming involved. I love saying things like that to the kids in the grammar schools, who are the cleverest kids; that they're the solicitors and barristers of the future. And I also say to them:

"It's on your shoulders. You are the future pillars of our community. It will rest on your shoulders, not to allow us to be sucked back into the dark days of conflict. You will be the

government officials, the solicitors and barristers, the doctors and the teachers. It will fall on your shoulders. You are society's hope for the future and it will be your strength and decision-making that prevents us being drawn back into those dark days of the conflict again."

They're almost proud that I'm identifying them as our future.

I tell them, "You are our guardians of the future".

Coda

*They say that it takes seven generations
for trauma to heal.
What will our legacy be to our
great-great-great-great-great-grandchildren?*

These words were spoken as the last lines in *We Carried Your Secrets* by Kieran. I have been holding them close ever since. Like a talisman, they remind me that every bit of healing we achieve matters. That our lives touch our ancestors as well as our distant descendants, and that we may never know who has been touched by the ripple effects of the good we do in the world.

Now, after all these years, I believe in the power of Theatre of Witness more than I ever have. I've seen ordinary people heal deep trauma within themselves. I've seen that healing ripple out to family and friends. And I've seen it offer inspiration for us all. I've seen performers who were once overcome with trauma, become leaders and model pathways of empowerment for others.

I have also witnessed how Theatre of Witness offers an antidote to the familiar ways we most commonly absorb stories about our society. We know the bleak grey narratives and tropes that bemoan the divisive problems we face. We are accustomed to hearing and seeing rants in the media that present discordant politics, incivility, cynicism, inertia and violence as the norm.

Theatre of Witness offers inspiration that comes from modelling a world where people from opposing sides become respected colleagues and even friends. Where listening, care, and empathy are core values. And where deep truth-telling can open and heal wounds that previously closed us off from further growth. I see how this work encourages us to become free from the paradigms of war, hatred, and discord while presenting a path of deep relationship building and creative peace-making.

And even beyond the examples shared in this book, I believe the Theatre of Witness scripts and stories also offer a poetic possibility of lifting the veil between this world and the next. Perhaps they allow us to find that mythical fifth province of Ireland. The land of imagination. The land of freedom. In many ways this work can be seen as a living prayer for peace.

None of this is easy or quick. It takes a lot of bravery and time to dissolve the knots that keep us believing entrenched and divisive views about others from opposing backgrounds. The work is messy and non-linear. We say things we wish we hadn't, and we inadvertently hurt each other. But the performers have demonstrated over and over again how we can pick ourselves back up, reach out a hand to another, and try again. How we can forgive ourselves and forgive one another. How we can trust our authenticity and let go of all that holds us back. Over and over again.

I am deeply humbled and grateful for the opportunity to have had my life intertwine with these wonderful people who have taken huge risks for the sake of peace. I hope the legacy of their stories will continue to ripple out and inspire others, and that they will have a permanent place in the history of peace-making in Northern Ireland.

With love and awe,
Teya, January 2023

Addendum

Theatre of Witness
Guiding Principles

Trauma and Re-trauma
by Dr Thomas Spiers

Glossary of Terms

Acknowledgments

Endorsements

Thirteen Guiding Principles of Theatre of Witness

Thirteen foundational principles are at the root of every aspect of Theatre of Witness. They have been the lifeblood of this art form since its inception; so woven into the work that I never even thought of them as guiding principles. Yet they only came into fruition on paper when one day a student suggested I write down what she had gleaned as the foundational teachings. Right from the start they seemed to fly from my pen with ease. It was then that I realised these principles had always been there - holding, influencing and supporting the process of creating this work.

Re-reading them, I am once again struck by how the Theatre of Witness form lies at the intersection between art, sociology, justice, history, psychology and spirituality. These principles arise in the space where they all meet. And although they underpin the practice of Theatre of Witness, I also find them to be guides for living a full and meaningful life.

1. Not Knowing

Not Knowing is at the very foundation of Theatre of Witness. We live in a culture where high value is placed on knowing facts, achieving, proving ourselves and being right. *Not Knowing* undercuts all of that, allowing us to see things fresh, to come in without an agenda or judgement. It means having a clean slate, being open and willing to meet people with little expectations of what the outcome will be.

Not Knowing also means being willing to work in an area one knows little about and trust that the stories will reveal what needs to be known. The performers who have lived the experiences being shared are always the experts. However, it's up to the director to choose carefully and wisely when selecting performers and stories. This means holding everything lightly, trusting the creative process. It also means there will be times when one truly won't know what to do or say next. It's fine to wait, to listen, to just be in the *Not Knowing*. *Not Knowing* is a state of open receptivity.

Not Knowing is also entering an improvisation. Like in a conversation, it assumes that deep listening will reveal the next step to take or thought to express.

2. Bear Witness

To *Bear Witness* means to 'be with' fully and compassionately. To be willing to be in the suffering with someone and to just let it be. It is sometimes the very hardest thing to do. Not trying to fix or make things different than they are, even if our heart breaks with sorrow. *Bearing Witness* asks us to open ourselves to the truth and reality of the moment.

Some stories are truly unbearable. Stories of horrific abuse, war, profound pain can bring even the listener to his or her knees. Sometimes all any of us can do is cry with someone. *Bearing Witness* means having an open heart and a strong centre, to remain clear and strong. To have a strong back and a soft belly.

Bearing Witness is infused in all aspects of Theatre of Witness. It's at the heart of the interview process when the interviewer listens 'with the ears of his or her heart'. It's embedded in the early group work when each participant tells his or her story as the group listens, then breathes in and out in unison. It's what the audience does communally when giving their attention to the performers as they share their deepest truths.

Theatre of Witness strives to *Bear Witness* both to personal story as well as collective narrative. In creating this work, it's vital to honour the individual and particular life circumstances of each participant, while at the same time giving focus to the larger historical, political, religious, social, environmental and/or spiritual group story shared by the cast. Sometimes what is most important is that each performer lends their personal story to the larger narrative of their people's story or plight. Thus the audience is invited to *Bear Witness* to the bigger story of a whole people.

3. Find the Medicine

Finding the Medicine is perhaps what distinguishes Theatre of Witness from other forms of testimony. It means to find the healing that resides somewhere in a performer's story or persona. In practice, walking with someone through his or her wounds until the place of strength, redemption or transcendence reveals itself. Without medicine, stories of suffering might just become a litany of distress, despair and victimhood.

In scripting performers' stories, the question must be asked: Why does the audience need to hear this story? "It's to hear the medicine." The medicine is where the inspiration lies; the point at which change occurs – of heart, attitude, behaviour or belief. *Finding the Medicine* can be a place of forgiveness, fortitude, survival or even openness and vulnerability. Often it's the place where victimhood changes to survival and denial into accountability.

Finding the Medicine can be considered as a re-imagining of what might have originally been a one dimensional or 'hardened' story in the mind of the storyteller into one with breadth, depth, paradox and space.

In groups, the medicine is often seen in the relationships of the performers, especially across boundaries. To see participants from polarised backgrounds or positions walk in each other's shoes and support each other offers great inspiration for audiences.

Sometimes *Finding the Medicine* is as simple as uncovering a performer's hidden talent and integrating it into their part. Or discovering an individual finds great joy or comfort when certain music or imagery is used. Medicine can be uncovering a moment of revelation, or a show of strength or compassion. Sometimes it comes from going right into the heart of a wound and finding light and beauty there.

4. The Blessing Is at the Centre of the Wound

Only by going through the darkest wounds do we find the light and blessing. As much as we all often want to skirt around the details and deep remembering of significant pain and/or trauma, I've found the centre of the wound always holds the pearl of wisdom or the open vulnerability. The blessing is often embedded in what seems unbearable. The fear and constriction one may have around a traumatic event is sometimes worse than remembering the actual wound itself. But this recollection must take place through a safe and supported process.

Sometimes the journey reminds me of travelling to the eye of the hurricane. In that quiet place of balance, around which great upheaval and tremendous waves of energy have been unleashed, lies a knowing. If one can accompany someone through the chaos to that place of equilibrium, a jewel is often revealed. It may be a sense of strength, a feeling of purpose or destiny, or a new insight. Whatever it is, the jewel possesses great potential for freeing up the grip of the wound. The expression of that awareness is often what most inspires audiences.

In this work, one often must go to the centre of a story in order to transcend it. As details, colours, sights, smells, sounds, feelings and thoughts are remembered, right through to the most specific, new meaning around an event can be found. Fresh imagery may emerge and through that, a sense of a broader, more universal story that is shared by people globally. It is within this new understanding of the universality of the wound that the blessing is found.

5. Deeply Listen with the Ears of Your Heart

Deep Listening means listening 360 degrees; with one's ears, eyes and intuition. Listen for the silences between thoughts. Listen for repetitions and blank spaces. Listen for body language and non-verbal cues. Listen to interpersonal connections within the group. Listen to your own reactions and monitor them carefully. Mostly it means listening without the judging mind.

There will be times in this work when participants reveal terrible acts they've committed, awful thoughts they've had, or even more challenging, demonstrate personal qualities that are disappointing. One's own prejudices and fears will get triggered. The director will hear things they wish they hadn't heard; know things they wish they didn't know. Within these unfolding stories, the task is simply to listen with as much of an open mind and heart as one can bear. Otherwise, participants will feel judged and probably become less open and more self-blaming.

It's also important to separate our own personal beliefs from the values and world-view of the person being heard. To make it safe for participants to reveal their deepest truths, it helps to hear the stories from their perspective. I believe curiosity is the antidote to judgement. So I ask the 'how', 'when', 'where', and 'what 'questions.

Yet through this act of active listening, care must be taken not to confuse judgement with discernment. In creating Theatre of Witness, it has been essential to make all kinds of considerations about who is ready to do the work, who will work well with others, and whose story has medicine that will be potent for the audience. Choosing participants who will not inflame, blame or make judgments about other performers.

Because the entire production is based on the lives, stories and personas of the performers, it's up to the director to assemble a cast who will work well together, inspire audiences and help to create a powerful production. This discernment process is quite different from judgement, which will almost always stop the creative and trust-building process of Theatre of Witness.

6. Become the Vessel

To *Become the Vessel* means to make oneself the most expansive and pure container possible. In other words, become the love you want to experience and express. Become vast, or as Walt Whitman described: "I contain multitudes".

Becoming the Vessel entails continually working on oneself, emotionally, spiritually and physically. To do this work well, it is critical to keep clean and uncontaminated by our own stories, opinions, prejudices and fears. I believe it helps to engage in therapeutic processes, both group and individual, and to read widely, become inspired, spend time in nature, and know 'the sweet territory of silence'. The more we can grow the capacity to hold, stay steady, and keep the largest possible vision of possibility alive, the more love, trust and connection will flow.

In many ways, this work is about allowing the state of 'being' to become more important than the state of 'doing'. Being calm and balanced, while at the same time retaining the ability to be passionate and moved. To that end, I highly recommend a meditation practice. The more that a director can become a vessel of understanding, compassion, patience and love, the more participants will open up and trust themselves in the Theatre of Witness process.

Lastly, to *Become the Vessel* means to follow our own life quest, questions and curiosity. It's vital to stay connected with that which has heart and meaning, and to look at this work as part of one's own journey. Crucially, this enables the themes and questions unearthed by participants to resonate deeply for the director also. Perhaps a participant's experiences will differ from the director's in the particularity of the stories and images. But underneath, it enhances the process if there is an underlying connection that deeply resonates with the director. Such connections fuel the creative process.

7. Hold the Paradox

Holding the Paradox shows how it is possible to hold ideas that may seem mutually exclusive, even incompatible. It involves going beyond opinion or belief and being able to accept polarised sides simultaneously; balancing good/evil, clean/impure, whole/broken, true/false, violent/peaceful.

We are not rational beings. Our experiences have a multiplicity of meanings. To *Hold the Paradox* means to accommodate them all, even if it seems unachievable. Not to expect consistency in stories, but to let things be, even in confusion or seeming impossibility.

Hold the Paradox challenges us to enlarge our sphere of understanding in order to contain these opposites. In essence, holding the story in a vastness that's bigger than either/or. When a multiplicity of meanings can co-exist, a new paradigm can be envisioned.

8. Find the Gold

To *Find the Gold* is to seek the theme or images that will be the hook or entry to an individual part or group scene. Gold can be found in the words or phrase of a performer during an interview or rehearsal that become a refrain or theme in the script. Sometimes the gold is discovered as a non-verbal symbol, movement, sound or interaction. This then forms the seed that flowers into a central idea. It's clear when the gold has been revealed; there's that 'ah ha' moment in the creative process and everything seems to flow more easily afterwards.

Finding the Gold is also about ensuring the imagery will speak symbolically. Powerful symbolism can encompass and envelop a story, giving it heightened meaning.

Lastly, *Finding the Gold* means to ally with the good, the true and the beautiful; all that will inspire and release the best in people. Find that 'vein of gold' which even amidst darkness and suffering will shine some light of goodness and hope.

9. Take the Problem and Make it the Solution

Often when creating Theatre of Witness, there are times when, as writer or director, I encounter a seemingly insurmountable problem. I used to try to bypass the obstacles, skirting around them, hoping they'd go away. Later I began to see that challenges are actually an invitation for creative thinking. So I often decide to take what seems to be a problem and, rather than try to 'solve it', turn it into a creative instruction. This guiding principle assumes that 'the problem' is actually an invitation to find a new, imaginative way of doing things that will actually end up being a gift.

10. Fall in Love

Falling in Love is the groundwater of Theatre of Witness. To do so requires experiencing and demonstrating the qualities of open presence, acceptance, unconditional regard and care for the performers. *Falling in Love* allows each participant to sense they can open their deepest wounds and dreams and share them in a trusting and safe environment. It also allows the performers to get intimate with their own stories, essential for scripting.

As the scriptwriter/director, I often use the analogy of swallowing and digesting the performers' stories in order to give birth to them in scripted text. It is an extraordinarily intimate act, which can't be done if there's resistance. The antidote is to be in a state of love. To open oneself to each participant and allow natural feelings of love and tender regard to come through, regardless of what acts the person may have done or not done.

Falling in Love is easier to do at some times than others. When I find I'm having difficulty tapping into that state, I know I need to spend more time in quiet reflection and prayer. I need to open myself to deeper states while being gentle with my own limitations. I need to ask for guidance.

11. Trust the Process

To *Trust the Process* is simply to have faith that the foundation and steps of creating Theatre of Witness will work. It means that, by staying true to the process, following the Guiding Principles and gently opening up into a receptive state, answers and directions will be revealed. Creative ideas will emerge, performers will support each other and carry the load, and the audience will respond positively to the genuine and honest story-telling.

Trusting the Process is our guidance to have patience and be willing to ride the waves of uncertainty, obstacles, conflict, confusion and doubt. These will always be integral to the creative process. Allowing these difficulties to just be and recognising them as a normal part of the creative process nurtures trust that they are manageable and will eventually resolve. When the director knows and reminds themselves this is all to be expected and natural, it is possible to hold the group with confidence and true support.

12. Everyone Is Me

Enlightenment and inspiration comes from learning to see oneself not only *in* others, but *as* 'the other'. It is about seeing ourselves as a refugee, a person who has taken a life, a survivor of war, a parent struggling with poverty, or a wealthy landowner. It's about being old, young, male and female;

Jewish, Christian, Muslim, Buddhist, Atheist or Agnostic. Through this practice, there is no one who can't be you; no one whose life couldn't be yours given the same set of experiences, genetics and karma.

This is a hard principle to practice and to get the heart around. The goal of seeing oneself in every human life isn't easy to attain. Perhaps it can only be an aspiration. But leaning towards this way of viewing the human condition helps negate judgemental narrow thinking and invites real empathy and love.

Maybe another way to say it is that *Everyone is Me* encourages communion with the other; dissolving the boundaries between us and inviting the heart into a vast landscape of interwoven connection. Keeping this guiding principle in mind while creating Theatre of Witness opened up the possibility of audience members humanising 'the other'. As a result, seeing 'the other' as self is greatly enhanced.

13. Express With Creativity

This principle is based on exploring through drawing, writing, movement, music, metaphor and/or symbolism to illuminate and transform an idea, image or feeling.

By playing in the realm of creative expression, a new way of seeing is free to emerge. Utilising a form that one is not well versed in can also bypass censoring, allowing something new and vulnerable to come to the forefront. Play, laughter, letting go and relaxing into a new form of expression is a powerful catalyst for something ordinary or monumental to be born. Imaginative expression is also a useful to tool to provide new meaning to difficult or stuck situations, in tandem with opening doorways of spirit, connection and joy.

Encouraging performers to engage in the creative process

during the early stages of making a production, can help the director *Find the Gold* or symbolism in the story. It can also help them identify the primary 'language' for a performer's particular story. Some people speak with their bodies, therefore dance and gesture would be primary. Others relate to singing or visual metaphors. Engaging in the creativity process early on can steer the entire project in a new and exciting direction.

Lastly, creative play can bring great energy and connection to a group. It can become the basis of ritual that will bind the group together, making it more bearable to share tragic and/or traumatic stories. Using the power of imagination can then transform the stories into something artistic and magnificent for performers and audiences alike.

Trauma and Re-trauma

Dr Thomas Spiers

Thomas Spiers, a psychotherapist specializing in healing from trauma was a student and mentee of mine during my residency in Northern Ireland. He created a Theatre of Witness production, Unspoken Love that was performed in 2014 and therefore has both a professional and personal understanding of Theatre of Witness.

Introduction

The personal accounts we have read thus far speak of courage; of finding the mettle within, of strength shared around and between people who have found a way to safely approach the darkest parts of our humanity and therein find inextinguishable light.

This is no easy journey. Rightly, concerns are raised that approaching the narrative of past experience has the potential to further injure individuals when there is little awareness or unfamiliarity with the insidious nature of trauma.

Here I will explore how Theatre of Witness is a trauma-informed practice, guided by a set of principles which create the conditions that not only protect performers, audiences and directors from reactivation of traumatic experience, but more significantly, foster an environment wherein post traumatic growth may occur.

Touched by Trauma

We are a body of tissue, muscles and organs, designed as armour to protect our existence. Trauma is the overwhelming shock that penetrates even the strongest human breastplate, cutting deep into our being, our nervous system and thereby disrupting our sense of identity. Trauma rends us asunder, shattering connection, separating us not only from others, but from our embodied self *(Levine 1997)*.

The word trauma means wound. This is a useful image, as wounds scab over, gradually heal from within, forming a scar that over time fades to become a distant memory of hurt, sometimes recollected in a story of derring-do. Yet wounds also get infected, requiring painful excision and specific external treatments. Thus offering a helpful description for those who continue to suffer and require ongoing therapeutic support.

Reminders of the Past: Re-traumatisation

Our concern here is re-traumatisation. Put succinctly, this is an awakening of past traumatic wounds caused by reconnection with those thoughts, memories, or feelings related to old occurrences, so that 'there and then' events are experienced as if actively present 'here and now'.

The legitimate concern expressed by those engaged in therapeutic work is that the overwhelming of a person's coping abilities by such reconnection exacerbates or stirs up traumatic symptoms. Thus perpetuating a sense of powerlessness and a fearful avoidance of re-experiencing crushing distress.

This fear of fear, experienced as panic, is known to lead to reluctance to access therapeutic treatment. Panic may cause some individuals to take false refuge in ways of coping destructive to their wellbeing, or, from their suffering, seek to harm others.

The Theatre of Witness approach

What it's not

It is important to state from the outset that Theatre of Witness is a dynamic performance art; it does not espouse to be a therapeutic modality. Those who are 'diagnosis and construct happy' may be sadly disappointed by this, but hopefully this work also offers a radical freedom from such constraints.

As a process of social justice, Teya's work rests wholly in the belief that stories told from our deepest vulnerability are both curative and restorative to individuals and communities. Stories are liberating them by offering convincing alternatives to dominant narratives that are often powerful socio-political constructs built around a notion of 'invulnerability', then used by us all, as either weapons or shields, to preserve the status quo.

What it's more like

Theatre of Witness is a conscious a-politicisation of story. By focusing on rehumanising individuals through depicting their grappling with life, it is creating what Stone (2005) calls a "lifeline between and within us". In witnessing how others live with their vulnerability, our own journey is infused with hope and compassionately enriched. Our aloneness dissipates as we discover that our struggle through difficulties may not be as unique as we thought. Through the universality of shared experience, we are welcomed back and restored into the human race *(Yalom, 1985 p8)*.

It is also true, that in line with many therapeutic processes, retelling the stories, particularly those of deep trauma, is a central part of the process of social restoration. Long experience and extensive research have shown that, while some individuals do experience symptom relief after talking about their trauma, others respond with an exacerbation of symptoms (van der Kolk & McFarlane, 1996). It is therefore incumbent on Theatre of Witness practitioners to assume clear responsibility for performers to protect them from re-traumatisation.

At the same time, Theatre of Witness is not storytelling alone. It is a theatre craft; an active reconstruction of real-life events elaborated over many months and turned from a poetic verbal account into an embodied visual communication.

Working with Potential Re-traumatisation

My own experience of working with life-threatening trauma and the very real potential for re-traumatisation was in creating a Theatre of Witness piece, *Unspoken Love*, with Stephen, whose father died beside him in the Enniskillen Remembrance Day bombing of 1987.

In the performance group, he recounted being buried beneath rubble. I heard him speak haltingly, dry-mouthed, gasping for breath; entombed within the wreckage. Tasting with him the damp ancient building reduced to dust. Seeing through his eyes the slow and sluggish shifting of debris from the body he could not as yet recognise as his father's. Sensing with him the muffled and muted outer world, catching the moment sound returned. Wandering with him "ghost-like amongst the living chaos", dazed and confused. Following his unsettled searching to finally return to that distinctively shod and broken body and the full recognition that his beloved daddy was dead. It was both an awe-filled privilege and harrowing experience.

Those who bore witness to Stephen's suffering were deeply moved, travelling with him to that dreadful realisation of his loss. It was a story he had never fully told, yet all who watched and listened came to know in some small part, for a brief moment, the devastating effect of what being in a bomb was like. For a time, transported by his enactment, we were there as he was there, but this time not alone.

Later in public performance, though entranced and touched, he and we remained simultaneously present. Together we moved through his moment-by-moment retelling of the experience; as observers, feeling the immediacy and reality of the story. We were not overwhelmed but transformed, because our compassion was aroused. And through this, he and we 'felt' some sense of healing.

This is possible because what audiences are seeing is the qualitative outcome of months of self-directed work. From the first seeds of selecting who is suitable to undertake the quest for performance in the first place, and, given the mercurial nature of trauma, determining who has the capacity to continue in an ongoing way. Performers learn to bear witness to their own story, supported by the cast as witnesses too, before eventually sharing with the audience.

In contrast, it is clear some forms of retelling can be harmful in terms of unregulated pace, intensity and unbridled exposure. Such unmodulated work may intensify trauma symptoms and block integration of past traumas. Embracing understanding from the therapy world, using a less violent approach, can be applied; gently 'titrating' - that is adjusting and rebalancing arousal so that people gradually assimilate their experience.

Risk and Safety: Dissociation

The 'symptom symbol' most commonly connected to accounts of trauma is *dissociation*. Understanding the dynamics of dissociation offers insight into how we might address many of the issues regarding fear of re-traumatisation.

Dissociation is defined as: A way of organising information... (that) refers to a compartmentalisation of experience: Elements of the trauma are not integrated into the unitary whole or integrated sense of self (van der Kolk, van der Hart, & Marmar, 1996, p. 306).

To elaborate further, all complex experience is organised into orderly gestalts, a *gestalt* being an organised whole that is more than the sum of its parts, through five core processes (Ogden et al; 2006).

For example, if I think of a beloved friend (cognition), I feel love (affect), my chest expands and my breathing eases (movement). I can imagine the smell of their skin and feel her warmth (five sense perception), while sensations in my core are soft, easy and warm (inner body sensation). This is a complex experience. It can be summed up as 'memory of my friend', where my core organisers coalesce in a coherent way to form a happy recollection of contentment.

Traumatic events can fragment this integration of experience. So that, for instance, a person can recount an awful event without emotion, or feel physically numb as they speak or 'banish from awareness' aspects of the experience. Such fragmentation may at the time have been necessary for survival.

Dissociation then is best understood as an innate mechanism to help us deal with overwhelming situations on a temporary basis. It is a useful coping mechanism which becomes problematic only when it consolidates into habitual patterns that shape our day-to-day living.

The situation is made even more complex in that for some, this protective dissociative response may become an entrenched experience which negatively defines their lives and relationships. While others may show resiliency and creative adaptation to life-threatening experiences. Critically, as Horowitz (1978) suggests:

"For some, the repetitious replaying of the painful memories actually functions to modify the emotional response to the trauma, resulting

in a gradual increase in tolerance for traumatic content".

As with Theatre of Witness, the emphasis Kerr (2022) posits is not "of mastering the trauma story — for example, remembering every detail as done with exposure therapy — *but rather* clients become aware of how traumatic memories organise their felt-sense of selfhood".

Paying attention to "a wider embodied vista" illuminates not only what happened, but also what the body and imagination did or wanted to do. What Pierre Janet termed "unclaimed acts of triumph — the scream that was suppressed, the shove or punch held back, the desire to run not acted upon".

Awareness of what did not transpire — what the body wanted to happen but could not do — becomes a central part of the new story about the traumatic experience. It does not matter that this story exists only in body awareness and the imagination (Kerr Ibid). Actions, movements and gestures of empowerment can become performative acts on stage.

The Problem and the Solution

If dissociation invoked by retelling or reconnecting with traumatic memories can have hazardous consequences; effectively working with dissociation is the key to successfully reassociating people to their traumatic incidents in a non-violent way that leaves them unhurt by the experience.

"A client is most at risk for becoming overwhelmed, possibly re-traumatised, as a result of treatment when the therapy process accelerates faster than he (sic) can contain"
(Rothschild, 2000, p. 78).

As Theatre of Witness practitioners, we need to be conscientious in observing the intensity of response as a person recounts their experience, and cautious in modulating their self-exposure to their own traumatic material during retelling.

We must employ our creative technique in mindfully slowing down the process of story sharing. It is essential that the storyteller is well-supported and resourced as they deepen into the details of their experience.

John Briere (1996, Briere and Scott 2006) developed a simple model of continuous reflection on traumatic responses during therapy; useful when undertaking any work that holds the potential of re-traumatisation.

Briere (Bicknell-Hentges, L., & Lynch, J. J. (2009, p4) postulated that the intensity of trauma reactions fitted three categories, or what he termed, levels:

Level One - The person, when engaged with their experience, shows minimal emotional stimulation. Their mood and external expressions, or affect, is flat and their body noticeably still. Their voice tone may be calm, and overall their behaviour appears to mismatch the memories they are describing.

Level Two - Indicated when the individual shows some affective stimulation but does not appear overwhelmed by this. Their reactions tend to match appropriately the traumatic content of their story, yet the person is relating both with the practitioner and their memories.

Level Three - The person is over-stimulated and feels immersed in the original traumatic experience. Symptomatically, this is indicated by gasping for breath, uncontrollable sobbing and regressive behaviours such as rocking or thumb sucking. Here there is clear risk of dissociation and re-traumatisation. The person may self-medicate, act out or drop out.

Daniel Siegal (2011) elaborated a similar model, here illustrated by Ogden and Minton (2006).

As with Briere (Ibid), they suggest that too little or too much psycho-physiological activation renders the person dissociated and their traumatic experience inaccessible to transformation. The task of the practitioner is therefore to hold the individual

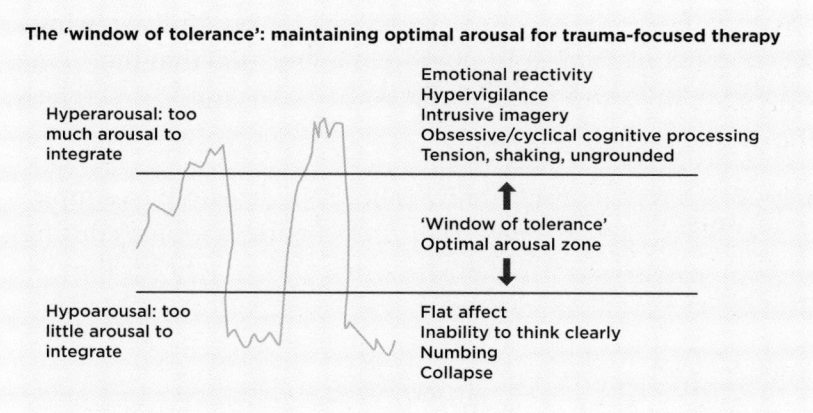

in a space where they are neither numb to experience nor overwhelmed by it, tracking their activation and containing their responses.

When arousal falls within this window [of tolerance], information received from both internal and external environments can be integrated (Ogden 2009).

Unmodulated activation allows dissociation to thrive. Too much arousal and the person will move into hyper (over) stimulation with symptoms of uncontrolled sobbing, hysteria, intrusive imagery, flashbacks and panic. Too little and they will languish in hypo (under) arousal where their affect is flat and they speak distantly about tortuous events with disquieting detachment, unmoved by their own suffering. From both places there is no hope of integration and healing.

As Theatre of Witness practitioners, we are engaged in opening a window of tolerance, letting in the light of other experience(s). We are creating a space within which the person can move accompanied toward their pain, to hear new sounds and voices including their own, to see new vistas of possibility, and to breathe and let something freshen their experience.

Staying Present

This leads us to the key question: how is it possible to retell the trauma narrative without re-traumatising the storyteller? This is especially poignant when directing someone whose experience is both physically and psychologically wounding.

It is a very practical concern. The apprehension felt undoubtedly springs from a fear of doing harm, either by unleashing forces that will overwhelm the person, or by being unable to helpfully contain or bear witness to the strong feelings that might emerge (Sazberger-Wittenberg 1970, p11).

We achieve this by using the principles of practice to guide performance co-creation. Employing the techniques of scripting and direction, we construct a framework to regulate arousal. We are endeavouring to take people to a new place away from a stuck story, but not into a void where there is no scaffold for the self.

Such skilful work requires building safety through trustworthiness, collaboration, empowerment and choice. All the qualities enshrined in the Theatre of Witness principles set out in this book. When applied, the thirteen guiding principles offer options for action that may not have been consciously present originally; burnishing unacknowledged strengths and gifts, and offering the opportunity for visceral connection with new roles and abilities.

This is all set within a compassionate relationship with oneself and others. It is this that characterises trauma-sensitive practice and exemplifies the strength-based approach underpinning the practice of Theatre of Witness.

A Look Behind the Curtain

How do we do this in practice?

Turning to practice, how does the Theatre of Witness practitioner endeavour to prevent trauma?

Our first imperative is that we are engaged in a process of Bearing Witness. We begin by witnessing our own telling, then share this with our group and eventually with the wider community in a progressive process of sensitisation to the full reality of our experience.

Ogden states that the first goal in the treatment of trauma is:

"To restore the client's capacity to tolerate and integrate their own thoughts, feelings, and bodily sensations, to bear witness to their own experience, to be able to process significant life events — past and present, painful and pleasurable, ordinary and traumatic — within a window of tolerance" (Ogden et al, p. 40).

It is foundational that the process of performing begins with a work of self-acceptance. This is key no matter when or what wounding has occurred in our history. Being kind towards ourselves even as we take up painful accountability is crucial.

The task of the practitioner is to ensure there is always the presence of a compassionate witness in the process of reconnecting with traumatic history. Otherwise the person is truly returning to a regressed state. If they are not able to hold this for themselves, then we must do so. This is why so much emphasis is placed on *Becoming the Vessel* and *Falling in Love*. While a lifetime's work, these guiding principles ask us to walk with people to embrace the despicable and the unbearable; to extend our capacity to hold wider the polarities of love and horror even if it strains us to new limits.

Healing in part occurs because the witness, as the matured part of the person or their ally, is present as they relive their past. The duty of their witnessing part or their partner is to ensure that the person always returns from visiting their history with a different, *"more creative"* conclusion (Sevlam 2022).

Bearing Witness does not necessarily require doing something, like offering analysis or evaluation, but rather rests in trusting the body-mind's innate wisdom that *There is Medicine in the Wound* itself. Think of the witnessing process as akin to holding up a mirror. The medicine is most often self-revelatory: a point of transformation arises, a new disclosure or awareness breaks forth, the possibility of redemption is felt, and the person fully accepts their situation. Or, put simply, a sacred moment occurs. Here The *Blessing at the Centre of the Wound* is found. The wounding is acknowledged, named and met. These are the points at which trauma is encountered without harm and with the possibility of healing.

The Scaffold of the Script

A principal way of regulating intensity during retelling is by using script creation. Theatre of Witness scripts are formed from the actual spoken words of the performers, recorded in writing contemporaneously as they speak. This occurs over many hours and weeks in individual interviews and facilitated by creative exercises undertaken in cast groups.

As each performer speaks, it is incumbent on the practitioner to listen beyond the story to the storyteller with a loving heart. To discern what is present and missing, notice what gestures are made or not, how pallor and posture change, tone and rhythm of speech quicken or falter; to notice if judgement arises and realise what would be present if one were not to judge.

In a process reminiscent of reconnecting the core organisers, the practitioner is weaving together elements both present and absent in the embodied telling of the story. Always trusting that the garment created will be more beautiful and protective than any single fragment of the historical experience.

We are doing this, not because we are working to resolve trauma, but because we believe that, inherent in this process of physicalised narrative, is an unspoken expression of the person's story, which possesses the power to summon compassionate feeling in ourselves and others.

The Place of Telling

I was pleasantly surprised to find in Briere's (2014) work this chart which reveals questions he might ask and actions he might take to enliven or dampen arousal in a therapy session. The eye-opening thing for me is that this form of exploration is so intuitively similar to the Theatre of Witness practice of script creation.

Increase	Ask affect questions, e.g. 'Tell me what saddens you'
	Ask for specific details of trauma, step-by-step
Anchor in trauma	Ask for sensory (visual, kinaesthetic, auditory, olfactory) memories of the event
	Ask about their fears
	Ask what's happening in their body
Decrease	Ask content questions not related to trauma
	Use calming voice tone
Anchor in the present	Stop client from talking and anchor in the present
	Repeat and rephrase what the client has just said
	Get client to open eyes and describe the current setting
	Use relaxation and breathing techniques in the session
	Ask the client about activities before and after present session or other events not related to the trauma

For example, a person could be gripped by what they anticipate we might ask.

"What are you not seeing?" or "What do your eyes want to see?"

These questions are posed from an imaginative standpoint, looking for gold, medicine and blessings – resources by any other name.

However, all is carried out with the intent of creating a performance piece, not to affect therapy. All the while the Theatre of Witness practitioner is tracking the pace and content of what is being shared: can this person deal with this just now? Can I hold lovingly what is being revealed? Always working in concert with the person as they reconstruct their experience and move toward the best way of having their voice witnessed.

At the simplest level then, performers look to the director for orientation. "Where am I in this process of retelling my story?" Therefore it is binding on the practitioner to have at least some sense that, while they are encountering the unknown, it is being explored carefully and in comparative safety.

A voice ...says, "*I know you're tired, but come. This is the way.*" (Rumi)

Sensitive direction points the performer towards the vital element of having their story witnessed. Performers are knowingly placing themselves, following spontaneous actions and gestures captured during their multi-faceted sharing. But under the director's guidance, they can do so in a deliberate way and be consciously witnessed.

Guided by the director's cues, they speak and enact their story, always with the witnessing audience in mind. A look here, a glance there, turning the head to convey another scene, but not so much that the audience cannot see their facial expression. Physicalising their tale in a way that is not contrived to form disingenuous feeling, but is constructed to deliver the fullness of their suffering and triumph and call out responsiveness from those observing them.

In this way, no matter how profound or harrowing the tale,

the performer is never alone in their experience. In fact, through the structures of direction, they are guaranteed a host of compassionate witnesses. The director then is a stalwart; a point of stability in a shifting experience. Their role is to arrange actions that support the process of being witnessed and build a strong connection with those witnesses. This grounds the performer in the living present, shielding them against unhealthy dissociation

Trauma-informed Theatre of Witness

Can it then be said that Theatre of witness is a trauma-informed practice, and if so, how?

Whilst knowledge of trauma and modes of treatment have flourished, becoming increasingly effective, the process outlined by Pierre Janet in 1898 has not significantly altered. His *phase-orientated-approach* set out here, remains the safe and enduring blueprint for all trauma-informed approaches (Treleaven 2018).

Phase I: Stabilisation and safety is focused on creating a felt sense of safety and stability. This is more than the idea, 'I feel safe'. It is better described as being felt in the contours of emotion, sensed in the body as a warmth and easing within oneself and in relation to others (Gendlin 1998). These are initial steps that equip people to contain and be with their experience so that it can then be processed (Levine 1999).

Phase II: Remembering and reprocessing trauma entails reconnecting with the memories of trauma and in doing so, understanding how specifically the story of trauma has become locked in the body and behaviour of the person. Because trauma often creates a smaller, more constricted view of who they are, the task is to renegotiate the relationship with that experience in a way that enlarges and empowers the person (Treleaven 2018).

Phase III: Integration with family and culture and normal everyday life is the intention to weave this new story into the person's narrative and to connect this to the stories told in their family and community.

The Theatre of Witness practice enshrined in the principles aligns closely to this phase-orientated approach.

STABILISATION AND SAFETY	REMEMBERING AND REPROCESSING TRAUMA	INTEGRATION WITH FAMILY, CULTURE AND NORMAL EVERYDAY LIFE
Not Knowing	Bear Witness	Hold the Paradox
Deeply Listen with the Ears of the Heart	Find the Medicine	Find the Gold
Become the Vessel	The Blessing is at the Centre of the Wound	Take the Problem and Make it the Solution
Fall in Love	Trust the Process	Everyone is Me

Stabilisation and safety - Listening and loving, untethered from assumptions and receptive to whatever the performer brings, creates safety and stability. This is engendered by a felt sense of the director's compassionate presence, of being patiently attended to and having the surety that whatever comes forth in the telling is held with gentle care.

Remembering and reprocessing trauma - As the sharing of experience unfolds, there is increasing potential for re-traumatisation. Peter Levine called on the myth of Medusa, the snake-haired Gorgon, when explaining traumatic response. To look at her directly was to be turned to stone. Perseus, the hero in the tale, is advised never to look directly at her. Instead, he used his shield to capture her reflection, and was triumphant in slaying the monster (Levine).

It is our inability to use the active defences to fight off or flee from traumatic events that leaves us frozen, triggered and reliving past trauma; literally petrified by our experience.

In the remembering and retelling of story; if it is to be more than a litany of despair, we must, as Pat Ogden (Ibid) shares, "restore acts of triumph" in the reprocessing. For change to occur, there must be some disruption in the story which is then enacted via the body in performance. This is a body, as distinct from the mind, or somatic, experience of empowerment, through playing a new embodied role. Fresh actions replace the old (Levine 1999 p238).

Bearing Witness conveys the message "I am here with you". This is a gift many trauma survivors never had at the moment of distress and often never believed they would receive. *Finding the Medicine* restores connection to those survival resources lost, forgotten or ignored in the moment of terror. As practitioners, we actively look for those actions or parts of the personality which were and still are seeking expression; trusting that inner knowing within the performer that they have a bigger role to play in life.

In this way, memory and medicine are married in the process. *The Blessing is at the Centre* of the Wound is perhaps the most daring principle, for it holds an unyielding confidence in the body-mind's desire to work in the person's best interest. It recognises that within us is a capacity or strength untouched by any outside harm, and once accessed, mobilises acts of triumph.

Trusting the Process is an extension of this deep inner belief. Holding fast to the principles will caringly allow creative coping to emerge. As Rumi advised, "Don't turn away. Keep your gaze on the bandaged place. That's where the light enters you."

Integration with family and culture and normal everyday life - Many cultures in conflict have no rituals for reconnection. Often their traditions are designed to reinforce othering and perpetuate division. Theatre of Witness aims to create a peaceful and just ritual for connection between divided peoples, where opponents work to empathetically understand opposing perspectives. The performers courageously face the issues at the source of their separation as they seek to build community.

Post-traumatic Transformation

That a process is truly trauma-informed will be evidenced by a sense of wellbeing and transformation in the participants. As is shown in the body of stories presented here, there is a danger in telling only a narrative of trauma; one that does not reflect the success of survival or the moves beyond powerlessness and despair.

Tedeschi and Calhoun (2018) open their review of post-traumatic transformation research with a quotation.

"Such pain must have happened for a reason."
(Salvadorian Political Prisoner)

Much attention has understandably been given to the negative impacts of trauma on people's lives. Less interest has been shown in researching the transformative impact of surviving traumatic experience and how healthy life-affirming changes occur as a consequence.

Tedeschi and Calhoun identify the key post-traumatic changes, including perceived shifts in:

- self-reliance and vulnerability
- recognition and appreciation of vulnerability
- sense of relationship with others
- greater self-disclosure and emotional expressiveness
- philosophy of life

This is what is presented in the performances of Theatre of Witness, not as a false Pollyanna construct, but a way of being that truly reflects the experience of post-traumatic growth by the performers. Moreover, as the ongoing role the participants play in peacekeeping bears witness to - they continue to meet suffering with compassion.

A Word on Witnessing

The lights dimmed. A charged silence formed in the warm dim light. Over the sound of sausages frying, a woman spoke: "Isn't he come in yet?"

I sat amazed. These are real people telling a story I wanted to hear, hanging on every word and action. I was entranced. This opening scene of *Juno and the Paycock*, seen when I was just 17, was my introduction to the convincing power of theatre.

To know how it feels to be touched by theatre in this way, is to acknowledge the impact of what is called out in us by witnessing drama enacted on stage. However there can be concern in some quarters, that watching performance may cause vicarious trauma. That is; the intense reaction of being exposed to someone else's trauma story or the details of a traumatic event.

Vicarious trauma, which mostly affects those in the helping professions, is said to produce negative changes in a carer's sense of spirituality, worldview and self-identity.

Thus the question arises: is Theatre of Witness a form of action that evokes empathy, whereby I imagine myself in the performers' shoes, or compassion, where I am challenged to take action to help others and find my own relief? It is this distinction, in part, that separates performance from a being a trauma-inducing watch into inspiring theatre. My strong belief is that it is the latter.

Cultures coming out of conflict have few rituals for reconnection between opposing sides. Most traditions have been established to solidify their separate identities and there are seldom neutral spaces for former opponents to meet.

Theatre of Witness has forged a form of ritual, for it creates a sacred space where peace and justice can meet in the shape of empowering stories told. A space where distrust and competition are exchanged for support and understanding.

Anyone who imagines this to be an easy process should try it!

Malidoma Some (1997) contends that a true community begins in the heart; "of coming together to do the right thing, even though we do not know what to do or where to start". Yet it is our intention to turn within, to heal the deep wounds and restore our inner power that is transformative (p83).

Often imprisoned by the prejudice of our cultures, choosing to leave behind old intolerance is not an easy path to take without the support and role-modelling of others. As Some suggests, from community we draw the strength "to make the inner changes impossible to make alone".

What audiences observe in a Theatre of Witness performance is a community built from opposing sides or excluded voices. An age-old ritual of sharing triumphant stories of struggles overcome, that in this instance pose a question, a challenge, a reflection: What will you do now about what you have seen and can no longer unsee?

Conclusion

"The end of art is peace."
(Seamus Heaney)

This gradual, presence-filled work of performance creation may give the impression that the practitioner is quite passive; doing little and effortlessly allowing the story to unfold. On the contrary, behind this calm scene lies a deep attunement to each performer's experience and an eye to safeguarding all that is happening. Yet all work is unforced and gracefully undertaken.

Re-storying trauma without due care carries a risk of re-traumatisation, particularly if there is a race towards knowing too quickly and fishing for any detail unnecessarily. The consequences of too rapid exposure can cause the return of traumatic arousal. Such haste can lead to a natural defensive dissociation in the performer in an effort to control or reduce the accompanying distress of reactivation.

Great care is achieved through the unique principles and practice of the Theatre of Witness performance creation. These work to guard against re-traumatisation by moving away from any emphasis on brokenness alone to the fullness of experience and lost qualities reclaimed. Intuitively, Theatre of Witness has followed contemporary understanding of trauma therapies in recognising that:

Without the balance of our non-linguistic world of images, feelings, and sensations, the seduction of words and ideas can keep us from direct experience (Ogden, Minton and Pain 2006, p. xiv).

By attending to the responses in the performer, stitching their story together alongside them, an intricate process of reconstruction of their experiences takes place. A witnessed enactment emerges that best illustrates their survival and triumph; re-traumatisation is prevented and those excluded and marginalised voices are allowed to speak. Heralding a new story that, beyond injury and despair, possibility waits.

Theatre of Witness has created a new cultural ritual that also generates a powerful therapeutic by-product.

The lives of the performers celebrated in this book, and the ripples beyond, are testament to the powerful qualities of post-traumatic transformation and growth exemplified in the witnessed plays.

About Dr Thomas Spiers

Dr Thomas Spiers, PhD, is a psychotherapist who was formerly Head of London Underground's Counselling and Trauma Service. For the last twenty years he has worked overseeing international employee assistance programmes.

He has supported those facing challenging times in Ukraine following the Maidan Square incident, people in Thailand after the Red and Yellow conflict, and those affected by the Japanese tsunami.

He has also assisted company employees during the Arab Spring uprising in Egypt, and the London bombings and terrorist attacks. He had the privilege of being mentored by Teya in the practice of Theatre of Witness. This was an award granted as part of the Peace III initiative in Northern Ireland. Thomas is currently completing mindfulness meditation teacher training with the Awareness Training Institute established by and affiliated to Tara Brach and Jack Kornfield.

Bibliography

Bicknell-Hentges, L., & Lynch, J. J. (2009, March) Everything counsellors and supervisors need to know about treating trauma. Paper based on a presentation at the American Counselling Association Annual Conference and Exposition, Charlotte, NC.

Briere, John (2014) Principles of Trauma Therapy. Sage Publications.

Gendlin, Eugene T., (1998 Sept.) Focusing-Oriented Psychotherapy: A Manual of the Experiential Method. Guilford Press.

Horowitz, M. J. (1978) Stress Response Syndrome. Northvale, NJ: Jason Aronson.

Kerr, Laura K. (2022) Trauma's Labyrinth. LK Kerr Books.

Levine, Peter A. (1997 July) Waking the Tiger: Healing Trauma: The Innate Capacity to Transform Overwhelming Experiences. North Atlantic Publishing.

Ogden, Pat; Minton, Kekuni; Pain, Clare (2006 Oct.) Trauma and the Body: A Sensorimotor Approach to Psychotherapy (Norton Series on Interpersonal Neurobiology).

Rothchild, Babette (2000 Nov.) The Body Remembers: The Psychophysiology of Trauma and Trauma Treatment, Norton Professional Books.

Selvam, Raja. What Is Embodiment + How Do We Do It? Trauma Therapy Network Host: Laura Reagan, LCSW-C | Date Aired: September 15, 2022.

Siegel, Daniel (2011 Mar.) Mindsight: Transform Your Brain with the New Science of Kindness, One World Publications.

Some, Malidoma Patrice, (1997) Ritual: Power, Healing, and Community. Penguin Books.

Tedeschi, Richard G. & Calhoun, Lawrence G. (2018 May) Posttraumatic Growth: Theory, Research, and Applications.

Treleaven, David A. (2018) Trauma Sensitive Mindfulness: Practices for Safe and Transformative Healing. W.W. Norton & Company.

Van der Kolk, B. A.; Van der Hart, O., & Marmar, C. R. (1996). Dissociation and Information Processing in Posttraumatic Stress Disorder. In B. A. Van der Kolk; A. C. McFartane, & L. Weisacth (Eds.), Traumatic Stress (pp. 13-30). New York: Guilford Press.

Glossary of Terms

Castlereagh: Controversial police interrogation centre in Belfast, now demolished.

Craic: Enjoyable social activity.

CS Gas: Irritant spray commonly used by police and military to incapacitate and subdue people.

Cup or plate: A way of asking if you are Catholic or Protestant.

Dissies: Dissident republican paramilitary groups

Fenian: Term for a Catholic of Irish ethnicity which can be derogatory.

H-Blocks: Another name for the Maze Prison.

HET: Historical Enquiries Team.

IRA: Irish Republican Army. A nationalist paramilitary organisation.

Knights of Malta: Members of the Orders of Malta, an international Catholic charitable organisation dedicated to alleviating suffering amongst the poor and sick. In Ireland they run an ambulance service.

LVF: Loyalist Volunteer Force. A loyalist paramilitary organisation.

Maze/Long Kesh/Kesh: A maximum security prison that housed suspected and convicted members of paramilitary organisations. Long Kesh detention centre became the Maze.

O Levels: Ordinary Level are subject-based academic qualifications achieved at age 16 after a series of exams.

P2: Second year of primary school for children aged 5-6.

Provo: Member of or relating to the Provisional Irish Republican Army.

Quartermaster: Military or paramilitary officer who provides and distributes supplies and weapons.

Ra: Nickname for the IRA.

RUC: The Royal Ulster Constabulary was the Northern Irish police force from 1922 until 2001.

Sinn Fein: Irish republican political party.

Slop out: Having no toilet in a prison cell, only a chamber pot which the prisoner must empty and clean.

UDA: Ulster Defense Association. A loyalist paramilitary group.

UFF: Ulster Freedom Fighters. A loyalist paramilitary group.

UDR: Ulster Defence Regiment. A former British Army infantry regiment.

UVF: Ulster Volunteer Force. A loyalist paramilitary group.

Wains: A local expression for children. Wee ones.

War of the Roses: Series of wars fought in 15th century England for the throne.

For more information about the Troubles and key events and organisations mentioned in this book, please go to:

The CAIN Archive - Conflict and Politics in Northern Ireland
www.cain.ulster.ac.uk

Acknowledgements

First and foremost, I want to thank all the performers who were in Theatre of Witness Productions Northern Ireland, 2009-2014. Each one gave so much of themselves and their stories. They allowed us to build cohesive productions from a variety of perspectives that had deep heart and soul. Although some cast members are not written about in this book, their influence was part of everything that has come from Theatre of Witness, then and now:

Adrian Duplak, Anna Kilgore, Anne Walker, Catherine McCartney, Chris Byrne, Everson Madumeja, Fionnbharr Ó HÁgain, James Greer, Jon McCourt, Kevin Kelly, Kathleen Gillespie, Kieran Gallagher, Louise Crossan, Loyd Ncube, Margaret McGuckin, Maria Young, Maryama Yuusuf, Paddy McCoey, Robin Young, Ruth Moore, Ryan Dougherty, Syd Trotter, Therese McCann, Vincent Coyle, William McKee, Victoria Geelan.

Pauline Ross and Eamonn Deane, were the most trusted and extraordinary partners and producers.

Very special thanks to artistic collaborators Aja Marneweck, Brian Irvine, Chris Byrne, Declan Keeney, John McIlduff and Margo Harkin who brought artistic excellence to all of the projects. And to The Playhouse coordinators who lovingly continued to guide this work forward: Mark McCollum, Nicky Harley, Emma Stuart, and then Liam Campbell, Claire Heaney-McKee and Kieran Smyth. Without you, this Theatre of Witness in Northern Ireland would never have continued to thrive.

Thank you to the team at The Playhouse for stewarding this book forward and acting as liason with the performers while I was far away, Siobhan Dignan for her expert editing, and Mark Willett for his beautiful photographs and design.

In 2013 -2014 I mentored two Theatre of Witness practitioners – Alessia Cartoni and Thomas Spiers. They produced two Theatre of Witness productions, *Unspoken Love* and *Our Lives Without You* - further ripple effects. Many thanks to the performers who shared their own stories in these productions: Sharon Gault, Stephen Gault, Jo McIntyre, Roley McIntyre, Aisling Devlin, Alice Teggart, Briege Voyle, Eileen Corr, Rita Bonner, Pat Quinn.

I am grateful for the many people who supported Theatre of Witness in our live productions and films: composers, filmmakers, assistants, advisors, funders, lighting and sound designers, administrators, photographers, puppetmasters, stage managers, facilitators, academics and friends.

There are many more who are not named here, and for them also, a hearty thank you:

Aine McCarron, Anne-Marie Langan, Brian Irvine OBE, Caitlin O'Neil, Cathie McKimm, Comas Sikhosana, Conleth White, Conor McIvor, David Grant, Davy Kilpatrick, Denise Crossan, Devon Nevotnak, Don Browne, Eamonn Baker, Elaine Forde, Emma Stuart, Fiachra O Longain, Fionnuala Deane, Gauri Rage, Gerard Deane, Guillaume Beuron, Hannah McKimm, Hector Aristizabal, James King, James Skelly, Jo Noble, John Donaghy, Justyn, McNicholl, Kate Moylan, Kathleen Campbell, Katie VanWinkle, Kathryn Stone OBE, Lee Smithey, Lenny Nelson, Maeve Sweeney, Magdalena Weiglhofer, Maia Brown, Mark Gallione, Mark Phelan, Martin McDonald, Max Beer, Maureen Hetherington, Megan Anderson, Michael Dogherty, Michael Kielty Jr. Michael McKnight, Niall McCaughan, Nick Wilders, Nina Quigley, Nikki Dunne, Pat Colgan, Peter McDonald, Rina Keyes, Roy Arbuckle, Samia Abbass, Sara Bratjbord, Sarah Gonzales , Stephen Hamilton, Steeven Petitteville, Tom Saunders, Tony Carlin, Victoria Keys.

Special thanks also go out to Bishop Street Friends Meeting, Holywell Trust, The Junction, The Nerve Centre,

The Playhouse, Queens University, The Waterside Theatre, and the Wave Trauma Center.

And to my friends here in the USA who have support me as I brought this book forth: Anthony Hinton, Dan Sipe, Ellen Murphey, Gene Early, Patricia Pearce, Sara Joffe, Sharon Friedler, Susan Teegen and the wonderful folks at Leaders Quest and my beloved women's group - The Cauldron.

Endorsements

"I am the ripple effect." These were the first words echoed from my performance in *We Carried Your Secrets* as a 21-year-old man, seeking answers in an estranged world.
Fourteen years later I reflect on the impact of Theatre of Witness in Northern Ireland.

When I started this process there physically was no 'Peace Bridge'. It's almost like I can't remember it never being there. Just like I don't remember a time where Derry didn't represent a place for storytelling and peace. I was honoured to also perform in *Release*, and I contributed to filming the *I Once Knew a Girl* documentary. I shadowed Teya for five years as a student.

Over these fourteen years I have had personal experiences where I can see how easy it is to hate, to crucify and to never forgive. I became parts of those stories. Almost unknowingly, aspects of these tales would be my future; child loss, issues around addiction and much more. This work is not only a reflection of the past but a cautionary tale for the future.

Theatre of Witness has given me deep compassion for those who are going through pain and empathy for those who are about to go through it. This work is like a lightning bolt to the gut which serves to find a path to healing. If people are willing to open their hearts and experience this work fully, they will find something of value, something close to healing, something close to truth.

Christopher Byrne
Performer, Theatre of Witness

Unlike the permanence of film, theatre is usually thought of as ephemeral – performers and audience share an intense experience for an hour or two and then move on. But the ripples in the pond run deep and the trace memories are hard to fathom.

Reading Teya Sepinuck's remarkable book, *We Are the Ripple Effect*, brought me back to the experience of each of the original Northern Ireland Theatre of Witness performances with a visceral immediacy. It will be a valued resource for all that saw any of these productions. But more importantly, it will allow many who were not so privileged to access these moving testimonies for the first time.

The book also evidences the lasting legacy of this seminal peace-building programme. At the time, many questioned the ethics of holding these courageous witnesses in an apparent trap of retraumatisation, in which they had to repeatedly relive their often disturbing stories. But again and again, in post-show discussions, the performers reasserted the profound benefits they found in bearing witness. There could be no greater vindication of the whole enterprise than the fact, so vividly recorded in this book, that so many of the participants continue to build on the original work in a wide variety of ways.

Those of us who believe in the value of the arts as an instrument of peace aspire to a virtuous progression from intervention to participation to agency, as those we work with internalise the skills and capacity to take full ownership of their own stories. This generous book shows just how brightly the spirit of Theatre of Witness has shone on.

David Grant
Senior Lecturer in Drama Queen's University, Belfast

It's wonderful to see the *We are the Ripple Effect* book come into existence. Many who engage in peace building in a conflicted society know lasting transformation requires a readiness to step out of comfort zones. They know too that meaningful outcomes can be both instantaneous and evolving.

Hence the importance of this book in bearing witness to the life-changing processes of renewal and emerging leadership that emerge when time is invested in people through thoughtfully crafted, truth-seeking and trust-informed processes and relationships. Some of the abracadabra of the Theatre of Witness work, for me, lies in the determination to bring together individuals and their 'stories' of lived experiences side by side, being unconfined by the oppressive polarities, hierarchies and social norms which keep people from realising our own authentic voice and often inter-connected experiences.

My hope is that this ripple effect continues, and in reading this book, we will teach ourselves something more about listening with an open heart and learn again to trust each other.

Ruth Gonsalves Moore
CEO, The Junction and performer in 'I Once Knew a Girl.'

Stunning, intimate, vulnerable, loving and steely strong - all elements masterfully mixed for the medicine of this work; soothing truth through testimony, again and again.

Denise Crossan, Ph.D.
Professor and Practitioner of Peace and Social Innovation,
Swarthmore College and Princeton University

We Are the Ripple Effect provides an important historical record, as well as a model for continued action in which Teya Sepinuck and former Theatre of Witness cast members are revealed as a resilient community of peacemakers. More than ten years after they created performances together, the contributors share scripted stories as well as reflections of changes in their lives and continuing community work. The book demonstrates ways that employing Theatre of Witness principles can offer a shared public space for healing from traumas that still reverberate due to The Troubles. As readers, we are invited to join them in fostering reconciliation across differences.

Sharon E. Friedler
Stephen Lang Professor of Performing Arts and Professor of Dance Emerita Swarthmore College, Pennsylvania USA

Having worked in the field of peace building for over 25 years, the lack of fairness and justice is, for me, the biggest obstacle to building sustainable peace. This book recognises the injustices for those living with horrific memories, trauma and pain by sharing the lived experiences of those from all sides of the conflict who have been impacted. While it is impossible to redress the hurt caused, there is a moral imperative to at least acknowledge the devastating consequences of the violence in all its forms, and this book does just that. This is an important book for all those invested in building peace.

Maureen Hetherington
Northern Ireland peacebuilder

In nature when a tree falls to the ground or an animal ends its life, the mycelium moves in to continue feeding life from what is decomposing. What happens to us humans when war, violence or tragedy seem to destroy all that we are?

Teya's compassionate work has allowed her to be a witness of the human capacity to overcome trauma by finding meaning in our personal stories and by sharing it with others, creating the ripple effects of collective healing. She has inspired many of us to be weavers of the 'mycelium of the soul' that connects us all with ourselves, with each other and with our deepest nature.

Hector Aristizabal
Theater for Reconciliation. Founder of Imaginaction

About the author

Teya Sepinuck, is the founder and director of Theatre of Witness, a model of performance that gives voice to those whose stories haven't been heard.

Since 1986, she has created and produced Theatre of Witness productions and films in the US, Poland and Northern Ireland. She has collaborated with refugees, healthcare professionals, immigrants, prisoners and their families, survivors and perpetrators of abuse, police, elders, and those who have lived through inner-city violence and war.

All Theatre of Witness productions and films are performed by the people themselves. The purpose of her work is to humanise 'the other' and bring performers together across divides of difference to model justice and peace. Her book: *Theatre of Witness – Finding the Medicine in Stories of Suffering, Transformation and Peace"* (Jessica Kingsley Press) was published in 2013.

Teya is the mother of two adult sons and has a long-standing meditation practice.

www.theaterofwitness.org

About the cover artist

Susan Teegen knows painting as an ally in healing and transformation through listening with color, form, beauty, pain and mysteries that are seen and unseen. She has alsospent over 30 years supporting creative and spiritual expression in individuals, groups and communities.

www.SusanTeegen.com